CW00568305

CHAPTER 1

Why Examine the Bible?

HAS the Almighty God provided a written guide for all mankind? Do you believe that the Bible is that guide? Or do you consider the Bible to be a "good book" written by wise men of ancient times—but no more than that?

There are people who are convinced that mankind's Creator inspired the writing of the Bible. Others are not convinced. Why not? Many of these have never personally read the Bible, so, at best, they have only a hazy idea about what it contains. Some persons ask:

> How could reading the Bible, which was written centuries ago, be of real value to me in this modern world?
>
> How practical is the Bible for people who need to spend their time working hard to feed and clothe their families?
>
> If the Bible's influence is for good, why have the "Christian" nations destroyed so many human lives in war?
>
> What about the discoveries of science? Have they not shown that it is unwise to view all the accounts in the Bible as actual fact?

Perhaps you have asked some of these questions yourself. But what are the facts? Have you ever made a personal investigation to find out? If not, you should do so now. Why?

SOUND REASONS FOR INVESTIGATING

It is not merely because the Bible is a very ancient book, parts of it having been written over 3,400 years ago. Age alone is not the major reason for interest in it. Nevertheless, mankind's history stretches back thousands of years. So, for any book to be the Almighty God's Word to all mankind, you would hardly expect it to be written recently, would you?

The Bible, available in over 1,300 languages, has a circulation of thousands of millions

Nor is the Bible's vast distribution the major reason for interest. Although, again, you would logically expect any book that is the Creator's guide for mankind to be available to people of all races, everywhere, would you not? The Bible has, indeed, penetrated every land on the face of the earth. It is available now, the whole or in part, in over 1,300 languages. Though few books reach a circulation in the millions, the Bible has been published by the thousands of millions.

As *The World Book Encyclopedia* (1966 edition, Vol. 2, p. 218) says:

"Almost everyone in the world can find at least parts of the Bible written in his own language. . . . No other book can equal its record. In one single year, enough copies were distributed to average forty-seven for every minute of every hour, night and day."

Impressive though these facts are, there are more important reasons for investigating the Bible. No matter who you are, no matter where you live, the Bible deals with matters that vitally concern you—your personal welfare, your happiness, your security. The possession of genuine happiness, with peace of mind, requires having sufficient good food, clothing and shelter. It must include protection from harm for oneself and one's loved ones. It must also provide for good health and long life. The Bible claims to show how these vital needs can be satisfied. Can we afford not to investigate what it contains?

Some may say, "But the Bible was written thousands of years ago. We today live in a modern, scientific world." True, but the ancient problems of mankind are still here, clamoring for a solution. Scientific advances have, in effect, reduced the distances between the peoples of earth by rapid transportation and communication, as well as by long-range war equipment. However, instead of lessening mankind's difficulties, this has actually increased them. Even though modern inventions have provided many conveniences, and lightened man's work, they have not solved the major problems of human living. When has the need ever been so vital to learn how to live at unity and peace with others? to know how to forge strong and loving family ties? to be able to make wise decisions in times of crisis? It is because the Bible comes to grips with these problems that it has such universal appeal. This is a powerful reason for investigating its message in these dangerous times.

An even greater reason exists. The Bible merits your examination because it focuses on the very purpose of life. Animals may be content with food, shelter and ability to procreate. Intelligent humans cannot be. For genuine satisfaction and happiness, their life must have a purpose. No doubt, like so many other persons, you have asked the questions: "Where did life come from? Why am I here? What does the future hold?" Since we have been given the ability to ask such questions, reasonably the Creator of man would provide satisfying answers to them. In every part of the earth there are persons who have accepted the Bible as the Word of God precisely for the reason that it gave them these answers.

Linked with this is the notable fact that the Bible itself openly says it is the Word of mankind's Creator. And it emphasizes this point over and over again. King David, writer of numerous psalms, for example, declares: "The spirit of Jehovah it was that spoke by me, and his word was upon my tongue." (2 Samuel 23:1, 2) The prophet Isaiah wrote: "This is what the Sovereign Lord, Jehovah of armies, has said." (Isaiah 22:15) And the apostle Paul said: "All Scripture is inspired of God." (2 Timothy 3:16) Were the Bible writers being presumptuous in making such claims? Well, if the Bible really is the Creator's message to mankind, then would it be honest on the part of these Bible writers to fail to credit Him as the Source? And since the Bible so definitely states that it *is* the Word of God, would it not be wise on your part to examine its contents?

There is yet another reason for you to examine the Bible and to do it *now*. According to the Bible, we are living in the last days of this trouble-filled system of things. Even world leaders freely acknowledge that global calamity threatens from many directions. But thousands of years ago the Bible pointed to such a time of global crisis, describing in detail the very things our generation is witnessing. The Bible gives reasons why destruction threatens and points to its source. It also sets out requirements for survival, and states that those preserved by God will be blessed with the opportunity to gain eternal life under righteous and happy conditions right here on earth. This prospect should appeal to those who daily work so hard to better their lot in life, only to find, at best, a short-lived happiness in this present system. When the strands of life wear thin in old age, it becomes clear that so much is presently beyond our reach, so much that we sincerely want to do, but must leave undone. If the Bible truly is God's Book in which he tells us how he will bring everlasting blessings to mankind, we should by all means want to know what it says.

Many, it is true, have declined to investigate the Bible because they identify it with the churches of Christendom. They note a marked loss of faith among many churchgoers and hypocrisy in the lives of others. But is the fault with the Bible? Or could it be that these churches are really failing to follow the Bible? In fact, how many churchgoers are there who have personally read the entire Bible? Church members, also, are urged to make an examination of the evidence in answer to the question, Is the entire Bible truly the Word of God?

PUT IT TO THE TEST

So, why not make an impartial investigation of the Bible? Put it to the test, as many others have done. Former chief justice of the United States Supreme Court Salmon P. Chase was one of these. In doubt about the Bible's claim that it is the Word of God, he decided to examine it as he would examine any matter in court, taking evidence for it and against it. Of the result, he said:

> "It was a long, serious, and profound study: and using the same principles of evidence in this religious matter as I always do in secular matters, I have come to the decision that the Bible is a supernatural book, that it has come from God."[1]

But why take somebody else's word one way or the other? Why not examine the facts for yourself?

If the Bible is what it claims to be, then those who try to discredit it are, in fact, enemies of Almighty God. Your falling victim to their devices would result in the greatest possible loss to you. If the Bible truly is God's Word, then you should follow its wise guidance and instruction, so as to gain benefits that are available to man in no other way.

We invite you, yes, urge you to examine the evidence. Determine for yourself whether the Bible really is the Word of God.

CHAPTER 2

Genesis Account of Creation —Fact or Fiction?

"IN THE beginning God created the heavens and the earth."

With these words Genesis, the first book of the Bible, opens. Many persons today believe that modern science has proved the Genesis account of creation, including those first words, to be in error. Even religious leaders take a similar stand.

For example, a publication of the Protestant United Church of Canada refers to the first eleven chapters of Genesis as "myth."[2] A new Catholic catechism from the Netherlands says the same chapters are 'largely poetry and legend.'[3]

Are these claims true? We need to know, for the Genesis account forms the very foundation of some of the key teachings of the entire Bible. Have you personally read that account? Why not open the Bible to the first chapter and find out for yourself what it says. Then compare what you read with the following information.

BASED ON ANCIENT MYTH?

Among ancient peoples, there were "creation stories." How do these compare with the Genesis account of creation? Do they form a basis for that account as has been claimed? Consider the evidence:

The main Babylonian myth of creation says that, during an insurrection among the gods, the god Marduk took the goddess Tiamat and "split her like a shellfish into two parts"; half of her becoming the earth, and half becoming the sky. Taking the blood vessels of another god that was executed, the gods are said to have fashioned mankind. (*Ancient Near Eastern Texts,* by Pritchard, pp. 67, 68) Among the Egyptians, one myth said that the sun-god Ra created mankind from his tears.

Now, what does the Genesis account in the Bible say? First, it says, God created "the heavens and the earth." Then he proceeded to prepare the earth for human habitation. At the beginning of this activity he 'caused light to be' for the planet earth. Then he formed an expanse above the surface of the globe, with waters beneath the expanse and waters above the expanse. Next, dry land, continents and other land masses, appeared above the surface of the global sea, and vegetation and fruitful trees were made to grow. Following this, 'luminaries came to be in the expanse,' to mark off seasons, days and years. Then came the creation of marine life and of winged creatures. After this, land animals were made, and finally God formed man from the dust of the ground.—Genesis 1:1-28; 2:7.

Compare this account with the myths referred to before. How reasonable is it to claim that the Genesis account is based on those myths? Says Professor J. A. Thompson: "It [the Genesis account] is a lofty, dignified statement devoid of those coarser elements that are to be found in the non-biblical creation stories."[4] Really, comparing the Genesis account with these myths is like comparing a palace with a pigsty. True, both structures have walls, but there the similarity ends.

And what about the shape of the earth? Does the Bible agree with any of the myths of the Middle Ages, saying that the earth is flat? Or does it include myths such as the one from an ancient tribe of India which represented the earth as resting on the backs of elephants that stood on a huge turtle that rested on a cobra? By no means. Of God, the Bible long ago said:

> "He is stretching out the north over the empty place, hanging the earth upon nothing." "To whom can you people liken God? . . . [He] is dwelling above the circle of the earth."—Job 26:7; Isaiah 40:18, 22.

Though the Bible writers had not circled the earth in a spacecraft or viewed it from the vicinity of the moon, yet their description was completely accurate, free from the influence of ancient mythology.

Earth as viewed by astronauts circling the moon. It could be seen that, as the Bible said thousands of years ago, the earth is round and hangs "upon nothing."

THE ORIGIN OF THE UNIVERSE

But what about scientific discoveries concerning the origin of the universe? Have they not proved the Genesis account to be outdated and inaccurate? Some persons think so and some scientists at least intimate that. For example, the noted British astronomer Fred Hoyle, in his book *The Nature of the Universe* (called by some "the Bible in its field"), says:

> "I think it can hardly be denied that the cosmology [study of the universe] of the ancient Hebrews is only the merest daub compared with the sweeping grandeur of the picture revealed by modern science. . . . it is quite clear that they were completely ignorant of many matters that seem commonplace to us."—1960, p. 137.

Obviously, modern astronomers have certain technical advantages over Moses, who recorded the Genesis account. That is, they have huge telescopes with 100- and 200-inch focusing mirrors and radio telescopes that "see" even farther than the light-receiving ones.

With all this equipment, what has modern science found out about the origin of the universe? Can they tell us anything that the Genesis account does not or that proves it to be wrong?

In plain words, eminent British astronomers F. D. Kahn and H. P. Palmer begin their 1967 book *Quasars* with this statement:

> "We are almost completely ignorant about the early history of the Universe."

Can this be true? Surely scientists must have some idea about the origin of the universe. Yes, they do; in fact, they have three different ideas, popularly called the "Big Bang Theory," the

"Steady State Theory," and the "Oscillating Theory."*

Would you feel greater confidence in the Genesis account if it coincided with one of these modern theories, say the "Steady State Theory"? If so, how would your confidence have been affected by this news report from *Science Digest* of December 1965?

> "British Astronomer Fred Hoyle, foremost proponent of the steady-state theory of the universe, has admitted that he may have been wrong for the last 20 years about how the universe began."

Then, would one of the other two theories perhaps be more reliable? Consider what scientists R. M. Harbeck and L. K. Johnson say of all three theories in their book *Earth and Space Science:*

> "None is better than the others. You, the reader, can choose the one you like best, or you can reject them all."—1965, p. 224.

Actually the Genesis account goes far beyond the confused theories of twentieth-century science. How so? They do not come to grips with the major question: Where did the original matter or matter-producing energy come from to form the universe in the first place? But the Bible answers that question.

SOURCE OF ENERGY AND MATTER

Swedish physicist Hannes Alfvén of the Royal Institute of Technology in Stockholm comments that the proponents of the Big Bang Theory

* The "Big Bang Theory" is that the universe resulted from the explosion of a single lump of matter and that it is continually expanding. The "Steady State Theory" is that the universe has always had its present structure and that matter is continually being formed. The "Oscillating Theory" is that the universe regularly expands and contracts over periods of thousands of millions of years.

Scientists admit: "We are almost completely ignorant about the early history of the Universe." "We don't know how the universe 'originally' arose."

"turn extremely vague when asked about what happened before the big bang. Sometimes they suggest that a prior universe existed. . . . But just as often we are led to believe that nothing prior existed." Putting the matter bluntly, he states:

> "We don't know how the universe 'originally' arose, and perhaps we shall never know for sure." —*The Worlds—Antiworlds*, 1966, pp. 3, 17, 18.

Is it reasonable, then, to contend that the person who puts faith in God's creation of the universe as related in Genesis is credulous whereas the person who prefers some modern theory is scientific? Note this comment by science lecturer Allan Broms in his book *Our Emerging Universe*. Of the main advocate of the Steady State Theory, Broms says:

> "He does not tell us how this new matter comes into being, but asks us (at least for the time being) to take its gradual creation on faith (scientific faith, that is), which of course means that we will take it all back the instant any positive fact gives us the slightest excuse. . . . And when we look dubious over taking so much on faith, he properly reminds us that we ourselves have no way of explaining how matter otherwise came to be . . . and that we are taking the Big Bang [theory] itself very nearly on faith."—1961, p. 18.

Really it is a question of deciding whether to put faith in the record of the Bible, which has never had to be updated, or credulously to follow shifting human theories.

Interestingly, there seems to be one point on which most modern scientists agree. Following Einstein's equation, they hold that just as matter can be converted into energy, so energy can be converted into matter. If this is so, it would mean that an intelligent Source of tremendous energy would have no problem in producing a material universe. The Bible speaks of such a Source:

> "Raise your eyes high up and see. Who has created these things? It is the One who is bringing forth the army of them even by number, all of whom he calls even by name. Due to the abundance of dynamic energy, he also being vigorous in power, not one of them is missing."—Isaiah 40:26.

The Bible speaks of that One as Jehovah God. —Jeremiah 10:10-12.

THE SIX DAYS

What, then, about the age of the universe? *Science Year* of 1968 speaks of the "birth date of the chemical elements" as being "from 7 to 15 billion years ago." But does not the Genesis account say that, about six thousand years ago, the universe was created in just six days?

No, the six "days" of the Genesis account are used only in connection with the planet Earth, *not the universe*. The Bible does not say how long ago the material that makes up this planet came into existence. The six "days" relate only to the preparation of the already existing planet as a home for mankind. Just how much time passed between the "beginning" of the creation of the material universe as recounted in verse 1 and the start of the first "day" described in verses 3 and 4 is not stated. So, by its very silence on when the "beginning" took place, the Bible allows for present estimates of the age of the universe or for any future revisions of such estimates.

"Nevertheless," some may say, "even the idea of this planet passing from a 'formless and waste' condition to its present form with continents, forests, plants, animals and men, all in just six twenty-four-hour days—this *still* is incredible!" But where does the Genesis account say that the six days were *twenty-four hours* each? Though some religious groups teach this, the Genesis account does not say it. You yourself use the expression "day" in a broad sense when you speak of your "grandfather's day." Likewise, the Bible often uses the word "day" in a broad sense. —Genesis 2:4.

Keep in mind that the works spoken of in the first chapter of Genesis are those of God, not of man. Man did not come into existence until the end of the period discussed. So, is it not reasonable that the time periods mentioned here are those of God, instead of those used by men? Are God's "days" of work controlled by the rotation of this globe? Obviously not. Of God, the

Bible says: "One day is with Jehovah as a thousand years and a thousand years as one day." (2 Peter 3:8) And that even to God a "day" can have more than one meaning is seen when comparing this text with Psalm 90:4, which says: "A thousand years are in your eyes [not a full day] but . . . as a watch during the night."

So it is plain that the word "day" can be used to refer to a twenty-four-hour day, a person's lifetime, 1,000 years or even longer. In fact, on the basis of the length of the seventh "day," there is reason to believe that each creative period or "day" was 7,000 years in length.

EARTH'S EARLIEST HISTORY

Should we look to modern science to establish the correctness of the Genesis account of the earliest stages of earth's history? No, and for very good reasons. Modern science is still trying to find its own explanations for these very matters. As geophysicist Arthur Beiser says:

> "While knowledge of the earth's size and shape is as ancient as Greek geometry and as modern as [Cape Kennedy's] rockets, man's understanding of the planet's origin—and its exact composition—is notoriously imprecise. . . . [How] continents came into being . . . is one of the most difficult questions that one can ask about the earth, . . . There are many more hypotheses than there are continents—nearly as many as there are geologists."[5]

This uncertainty is stated even more frankly by Professor J. H. F. Umbgrove, who says:

> "But why should we not enter [this field] if everyone who wants to join us in our geopoetic expedition into the unknown realm of the earth's early infancy is warned at the beginning that probably not a single step can be placed on solid ground?"[6]

As with the origin of the universe, so too with

earth's early history, twentieth-century science is still groping in the dark. How, then, can its theories qualify as a standard by which to measure the accuracy of the Genesis account?

True, the Genesis account of creation is very simple. Does that weaken it in your eyes, making you feel that it is "unscientific"? It should not. Why not? Because even modern scientists are obliged to recognize the value and strength of simplicity. The book *Earth's Shifting Crust* says that in Einstein's philosophy of science "simplicity was a prime consideration." The Genesis account is notable for its simplicity and yet for its providing a suitable answer to the major questions of mankind.

Remember, too, that knowledge is continually increasing, and new discoveries cause drastic changes in scientific views once thought to be final. As professor and natural scientist Merritt Stanley Congdon cautions:

> "Science is tested knowledge, but it is still subject to human vagaries, illusions and inaccuracies. . . . It begins and ends with probability, not certainty. . . . There is no *finality* in scientific inferences. The scientist says: 'Up to the present, the facts are thus and so.' "[7]

With this in mind, let us consider some of the criticisms raised against the Genesis account.

WHAT TOOK PLACE ON DAYS ONE AND FOUR

A frequent objection is that the Genesis account says God produced light on the "first day" but that it was not until the "fourth day" that God made the sun, moon and stars. (Genesis 1:3-5, 14-19) How can this be explained?

First, we need to get the whole picture there presented. Neither "day" deals with the actual *creation* of the sun, moon and stars. The Hebrew word for "make" (*'a·sah'*) used with regard to the fourth "day," is not the same as the word for "create" (*ba·ra'*) used in verses 1, 21 and 27. Genesis 1:1 shows that the "heavens," which include the sun, moon and stars (compare Psalm 8:3; 19:1-4), were already *created* before the "first day" even began. Yet, prior to the "first day" the earth itself was in darkness. (Genesis 1:2) How could this be, since the sun was there and the earth was revolving around it?

The Bible does not state what prevented the sun's rays from reaching the planet at that point. It is known that within the Milky Way, the galaxy in which our solar system operates, there are dark regions caused by cosmic dust and perhaps gases ("space smog") that only radio telescopes can penetrate. Whatever the cause of the darkness enshrouding the earth prior to the "first day" or preparatory period, that "day" saw the cause removed. Now, instead of being in total darkness, the spinning planet always had one-half bathed in light while the other half was in darkness.

What, then, happened on the "fourth day"? Remember that between the "first day" and the "fourth day" a new factor entered the picture. During the second creative period the "expanse" of atmosphere came into existence. The record shows that this expanse, in which winged creatures would later fly, resulted from a dividing or separating of the waters, some now lying beneath the expanse and other waters being above the expanse. Note that it was *in this expanse* that the luminaries 'came to be' on the "fourth day." (Genesis 1:6-8, 20) How did this happen?

That there were 'waters above the expanse' is evidently the key to understanding the matter. These waters likely blocked the entry of light rays within the expanse. In fact, the book of Job, in describing the earth's formation, at one point speaks of it as having "the cloud as its garment and thick gloom as its swaddling band."—Job 38:4-9.

To illustrate: One planet in our solar system, Venus, is completely blanketed by an unbroken layer of clouds. Even with their powerful telescopes, astronomers have never seen its surface. Though Earth's "swaddling band" may have been of different composition, the present state of Venus at least illustrates what may have been the condition of its neighbor planet Earth up until the "fourth day."

One thing is certain: A notable change took place in that fourth period. We have no way of knowing exactly what processes were involved. The Bible does not state. Scientists cannot tell us. But now God evidently caused the "swaddling band" high above the earth to become translucent, thus dispelling the darkness beneath. So, by God's creative force the sun, moon and stars were now "made" to be visible from within the earth's atmosphere, "to shine upon the earth." (Genesis 1:15) Man, when later created, would thus be able to use them in measuring time. Now sunrise and sunset would provide a demarcation between day and night. The lunar phases would mark off the months. The sun's position in the sky, as it seemed to move toward the south or toward the north, would mark off the seasons and years.

VEGETATION ON THE "THIRD DAY"

On the third creative "day," following the appearance of the land areas and the formation of seas, the Creator caused the earth "to put forth grass, vegetation bearing seed according to its kind and trees yielding fruit, the seed of which is in it according to its kind."—Genesis 1:9-13.

The question is raised: How could this vegetation grow and survive for thousands of years until the coming of the "fourth day" and the appearance of the sun? What about photosynthesis, that is, the process by which the green substance in plants called chlorophyll reacts to light and converts water and carbon dioxide into life-sustaining food? Is the appearance of vegetation on the third creative period out of order?

Here again it is evident that men cannot say with any certainty what was or was not possible at that early period of earth's history. Consider a report from *Science News Letter* of August 25, 1962, under the headline "Lightless Photosynthesis." After showing that biochemists Kunio Tagawa and Daniel Arnon succeeded in 'eliminating the need for light in a key energy-transforming reaction of the photosynthetic process' in spinach leaves—"a feat that would have been considered impossible under the theories . . . that prevailed until recent years"—the article states:

> "In place of light, they supplied the initial energy 'kick' with hydrogen gas, known to be a powerful electron supplier."
>
> "The result was the production of reduced pyridine nucleotide by chloroplasts (that is, the build-up of a key store of chemical energy) entirely in the dark."

This experiment only involved causing a "portion of the primary photochemical act without light." It may not coincide with or even approximate what the Creator accomplished during the third creative period. Yet it illustrates the point that things often called "impossible" turn out to be possible—when certain previously unknown factors are brought into action. Who can say what the atmospheric conditions on earth were at the time vegetation was brought forth or what forces were then at work? How wise is it to deny the correctness of the Genesis account when there are so many things that are not known? As Russian-born biochemist and physicist Eugene Rabinowitch stated:

> "In photosynthesis, we are like travelers in an unknown country around whom the early morning fog slowly begins to rise, vaguely revealing the outlines of the landscape."[8]

The horizon of human knowledge will continue to widen. Already it has shown many critics of the Bible to have been too narrow in their viewpoint.

So, too, with pollination. The fact that the creation of vegetation (on the "third day") evidently preceded the creation of insects is no reason for doubting the truthfulness of the Bible account. There are numerous ways in which plants may be pollinated. Note the following by Professor J. D. Meeuse in the 1961 publication *The Story of Pollination:*

> "First of all, in spite of Darwin's famous dictum ('Nature tells us in the most emphatic way that she abhors perpetual self-fertilization'), it is a fact that successful self-fertilization occurs with great regularity in a large number of plants, including important agricultural species such as peas. Then there is pollination by the wind in grasses, ever-

greens, and various spring-flowering deciduous trees. In a few cases, water acts as the helper, and finally there are some very exceptional cases where no pollination of any sort is required."—P. 209.

Additionally, he shows that even within the same family of trees, including maples, oaks and chestnuts, one variety may be wind-pollinated while others are insect-pollinated. Who knows which varieties were the earliest ones to exist? And why should we doubt that the One who created the vegetation in all its amazing diversity could also see to it that, before the appearance of insects, the plants were pollinated in one of the above ways or in still other ways that men have not yet discovered?

One decisive factor should not be overlooked. The Genesis account shows that the spirit or active force of God was operating in a marvelous variety of ways during those creative days. —Genesis 1:2.

GENESIS AND THE GEOLOGISTS' "RECORD OF THE ROCKS"

After mentioning the bringing forth of vegetation and the making of the celestial bodies visible, the Genesis account describes the creation of marine creatures, birds and land animals on the fifth and sixth "days."—Genesis 1:20-25.

Even though the Bible allows thousands of years for these creative "days," this will not satisfy some persons. They have read statements by geologists and others that earthly life, both vegetable and animal, has been in existence for hundreds of millions of years. What about this? What is the so-called "record of the rocks" that supposedly proves this claim?

The average person, reading a book on geology,

may be mystified and even impressed by strange terms such as Cambrian, Devonian and Carboniferous. He may not realize that these periods so named, as well as the others referred to by geologists, are basically the product of human interpretations. Note what a university professor of geology states in the textbook *Outlines of Geology:*

"Much of the information contained in this book is within the well-lighted zone of proved fact. But no one ought to embark upon a study of even the elements of geology without realizing that we quickly pass from fact into a twilight zone of inference in which we can say, not 'This is true,' but only 'Probably this is true,' and that thence we pass into a region of darkness lit here and there by a guess, by speculation. Speculation is a legitimate . . . thought process just as long as the thinker fully realizes that he is only speculating. But when he speculates, and at the same time persuades himself (and also, alas, his listeners) that he is drawing sound inferences, then knowledge does not progress. The reader of this book should remember at every page . . . that 'We do not know' must be said or implied at nearly every turn, and finally that *what we do not know at present* would fill an indefinite number of volumes."—1949, p. 12.

Consider, then, some of the evidence about the "record of the rocks." When confronted with a geologists' chart of the earth's time periods one might think that the geologists find such a record practically anywhere they dig down deep enough. Is that so? By no means! The book *The Earth Our Home* says:

"The record of the rocks is confused and broken, with many parts of it missing altogether."—1957, p. 30.

Another science publication tells us:

"There is no single place on the earth where all the rocks in this series can be found. In any one place, some of them have been destroyed. Geologists studied the best examples of rocks in many places. Then, after long and patient work, they pieced the series of rocks together."[9]

Since geologists have never found a complete series, it is obvious that they decided the order in which to place the rocks gathered from many places and they also assigned the time they thought best to allow for each period. So, the millions of years that each of these geological periods is supposed to cover are arbitrary figures of the geologists. How did they arrive at them? Primarily by the length of time they calculated would be necessary to conform to the theory of evolution.*

Recently, however, geologists claim that new dating methods confirm their estimates of millions of years for certain geological periods. These methods use certain elements such as radiocarbon, radioactive potassium, uranium and thorium, which give off radioactive particles. Scientists measure the amount of radioactive material and the product resulting from its "decay" or loss of radioactivity. Then they compare this with what is believed to be its rate of "decay." Assuming that nothing has disturbed this substance since it was formed and that the "decay" rate has always been consistent, they use this information to calculate the age of the substance in which the radioactive material is found. How reliable are such radioactive "clocks"?

To measure time there must be a starting point, a "zero point" from which the clock begins

---

* For a full discussion of the evidence refuting the theory of evolution, see the book *Did Man Get Here by Evolution or by Creation?*

to measure. Showing the need for determining the original concentration of such radioactive material to be able to ascertain when the clock was at zero, astronomer Allan R. Sandage in *Science Year* of 1968 says:

> "We know the amounts of these elements in the universe today. We can read the time if we can find how these elements formed, for we can then estimate how much of each was made."—P. 64.

Can scientists determine this key point? Allan Sandage says, No. Why? "Because no astrophysicist was present at their creation." And Professor of Metallurgy Melvin A. Cook states:

> "Unfortunately, one may only guess these concentrations [of radioactive materials], and the age results thus obtained can be no better than this guess."[10]

Besides this guesswork in its starting point, what if the clock disagreed with other clocks and even showed signs of damage in its inner works? Note what the book *How Old Is the Earth?* says of the radioactive-decay time measurements:

> "The drawback with the [radioactive-decay] method is the lack of general distribution of radioactive minerals and the fact that these radioactive minerals have suffered such a large amount of radiation damage that they frequently show ages that are not concordant."—1959, p. 105.

It is not surprising, then, that the radioactive-decay method of dating has produced erroneous results. As an example of the confusion resulting from the use of this damaged "clock," a special report from Romania to the New York *Times*, March 26, 1967, stated:

"For nearly 50 years, the dating of the Vinca culture has been an open controversy among anthropologists. A radiocarbon test of burnt wood splinters from the Vinca area in 1953-54 indicated that they dated from about 4100 B.C. But this date contradicted the evidence of rock strata, which suggested that the culture dated from about 2900 B.C."

And in other instances, possible errors of thousands of years are acknowledged.

Is a dating method that can be thousands of years in error and that starts with guesswork a sound basis for doubting the accuracy of the Genesis account? Would you be inclined to put trust in a clock if you were not certain that it had been set at the right time and if you knew that its gears were damaged?

ADAM AND EVE

Perhaps no part of the Genesis account has come under more attack than the part relating to the creation of the first man and woman in the Garden of Eden:

"And God proceeded to create the man in his image, in God's image he created him; male and female he created them."—Genesis 1:27; 2:8.

What is necessary to satisfy a person as to the truthfulness of the account concerning Adam and Eve? Does it require a copy of the *Eden Times* dated 4026 B.C.E. with a photograph of the act of creation in process? This, of course, will never be supplied. But what objection to the Bible account could a reasonable person have? Is there basis for doubting that there ever was an original human pair? Is belief in an original pair "unscientific"?

For answer, note this from a publication printed in Paris by the Educational, Scientific and Cultural Organization of the United Nations:

"All of us, if we went back far enough, hundreds of generations, would arrive at the same place—the base of the human family tree with the first *Homo sapiens*. . . . Our common ancestor could as well be called Adam, which also means man in Hebrew, for the familiar Biblical story foreshadowed the evidence of science that present men derive from a common stock."[11]

And another scientific publication, *The Races of Mankind,* says:

"The Bible story of Adam and Eve, father and mother of the whole human race, told centuries ago the same truth that science has shown today: that all the peoples of the earth are a single family and have a common origin."—1951, pp. 3, 4.

What has brought the scientists to such conclusions? Anthropologist M. F. Ashley Montagu explains:

"All varieties of man belong to the same species and have the same remote ancestry. This is a conclusion to which all the relevant evidence of comparative anatomy, paleontology, serology, and genetics, points. On genetic grounds alone it is virtually impossible to conceive of the varieties of man as having originated separately."[12]

The like structure of humans of all races and the fact that they can all intermarry and produce children point to our having descended from an original human pair, male and female. Why, then, should we balk at calling these first ancestors Adam and Eve?

The creation of the first woman as recorded in Genesis has been scoffed at by some. The account states that, while Adam slept, God took one of his ribs and "proceeded to build the rib that he had taken from the man into a woman and to bring her to the man." (Genesis 2:21, 22) Some persons may refuse to believe this.

All humans descended from Adam and Eve, says the Bible. "All the peoples of the earth are a single family and have a common origin," scientists acknowledge.

Yet they will read with great interest and seriousness an article such as appeared in *Life* magazine of September 10, 1965. It dealt with experiments on plant cells by biologists, and contained the following statement:

> "They [the biologists] expect similar breakthroughs with animal cells. It is thus not absurd to imagine the day when a single tiny cell taken from the skin of the world's greatest genius might be grown into a second individual who is in every respect identical."—P. 72.

So, some find more plausible a scientist's making a man or woman from even a single cell than for God to produce a woman from a rib. This suggests that, for such persons, the Genesis account would be more "acceptable" if the words "human scientist" were substituted for the word "God."

THE EVENTS IN EDEN

In reading the remainder of the account of the events in the Garden of Eden, one may again note its simplicity. But we have seen that simplicity is no reason for doubting the account's truthfulness. Most important, the account explains certain things that otherwise would be unexplainable.

No matter who we are, no matter where we live on this planet, we are all faced with the evidence that we have a common ancestry. The grand truth found in Genesis was restated by the apostle Paul in Athens, Greece, that God "made out of one man every nation of men, to dwell upon the entire surface of the earth." (Acts 17:26) This truth provides a solid basis for the long-desired goal of a united family of all nations and races.

Another self-evident fact that confronts us is the imperfection inherent in all humankind. This produces, not only sickness, aging and death, but also wrong acts, difficulties and errors; it contributes to crime, immorality and bloodshed. How did this come to be? Only the simple account of Genesis gives the explanation. It is worthy of your thoughtful reading.

NO HALFWAY ACCEPTANCE POSSIBLE

Is it necessary to believe the entire Genesis account in order to accept the Bible as the inspired Word of God? Or can one pick and choose according to his personal preference and ideas? The latter attitude seems to be the one preferred by an ever-increasing number of so-called "Christian" clergymen. As an example, after the American astronauts read portions from the book of Genesis during the first successful trip around the moon, what did the Episcopalian ministers of two of the men say? They quickly denied that the Genesis account is factual, one minister calling it a "myth."[13]

In contrast, Christ Jesus clearly accepted as fact the Bible account of Genesis. To religious critics in the first century, Jesus said:

> "Did you not read that he who created them from the beginning made them male and female and said, 'For this reason a man will leave his father and his mother and will stick to his wife, and the two will be one flesh'? So that they are no longer two, but one flesh. Therefore, what God has yoked together let no man put apart."—Matthew 19:4-6; Genesis 1:27; 2:24.

The Bible writer Luke, who states that he "traced all things . . . with accuracy," gives Jesus' ancestry from his own day back to Adam.

If the Genesis account is a myth, then just where, between Jesus and Adam, did the genealogy become mythical?—Luke 1:1-4; 3:23-38.

Further, Jude, the half brother of Jesus Christ, describes Enoch as "the seventh man in line from Adam." (Jude 14) What logic does it make to refer to any man as "the seventh" in line, if the starting point for the line is only a myth?

The learned apostle Paul did not doubt the accuracy of the Genesis account concerning Adam and the origin of sin. He states: "Through one man sin entered into the world and death through sin, and thus death spread to all men because they had all sinned—. Nevertheless, death ruled as king from Adam down to Moses, even over those who had not sinned after the likeness of the transgression by Adam." (Romans 5:12, 14) It is on this basis that the ransom sacrifice of Jesus Christ is stated to be effective on behalf of all mankind as descendants of Adam.

Those who reject the Genesis account may not realize that by so doing they reject Christianity. Why? Because the ransom sacrifice of Jesus Christ became necessary as a result of what Adam himself did. Whoever accepts the ransom sacrifice of Jesus Christ must also believe that the Genesis account is fact, because the one is the basis for the other. No halfway acceptance is possible.

So what does the evidence show? That there is every reason to accept the Genesis account of creation as fact. While it is at odds with certain *theories*, it harmonizes with proved scientific *fact*. It reaches out far beyond details of limited value and provides answers to questions of life that are of greatest concern to all of us.

CHAPTER 3

Was There an Earth-wide Flood?

BY THE days of Noah, the Bible record says, the earth had become "full of violence," as is also true of our day. What resulted?

The Bible relates that God informed Noah, "because all flesh had ruined its way on the earth," he would wipe out that violent world of mankind by a flood. Noah was to build a spacious ark for the saving of his household and all the various kinds of land animals and birds. Then, at God's command, the floodwaters fell, covering even the highest mountains. Of mankind, only those in the ark survived. (Genesis 6:12, 13; 7:1-24) Did these things really happen? There is strong evidence that they did.

Some persons will accept this account only if the Flood is viewed as merely a *local* one. But that is not what the Bible says. If the Flood had been local, why would not God simply have told Noah to move to another locality? Why all the labor of building a large ark for survival? If the Flood did not cover all the earth, why bring animals and birds into the ark to preserve all the different kinds? Animals elsewhere could have survived. And the birds could have easily escaped by flying to another area. So we must face the fact that to believe this account means accepting that there was a *global* flood.

THE FLOODWATERS —FROM WHERE AND TO WHERE?

Of course, you may wonder where such a vast amount of water could come from. The Genesis account states that during the second creative period or "day," when the earth's atmospheric "expanse" was formed, there were 'waters beneath the expanse' and 'waters above the expanse.' (Genesis 1:6, 7) The waters "beneath" were those already on earth. The waters "above" were huge quantities of moisture suspended high above the earth, forming a "vast watery deep." These waters fell in Noah's day.—Genesis 7:11, 12.

In the book *The Genesis Flood* (pages 240, 241), coauthor Professor Henry M. Morris of the Virginia Polytechnic Institute examines the scientific aspect of such a water canopy above the earth. He says:

> "The region above about 80 miles is very hot, over 100° F and possibly rising to 3000° F, and is in fact called the thermosphere for this reason. High temperature, of course, is the chief requisite for retaining a large quantity of water vapor. Furthermore, it is known that water vapor is substantially lighter than air."

Of course, no person today can know what the composition or nature of the upper atmosphere was in the ancient past. However, as Professor Morris goes on to say:

> "There is thus nothing physically impossible about the concept of a vast thermal vapor blanket once existing in the upper atmosphere."

The Bible says that, when the suspended waters fell, they "overwhelmed the earth so greatly that all the tall mountains that were under the whole heavens came to be covered. Up to fifteen cubits [about twenty-two feet] the waters overwhelmed them."—Genesis 7:19, 20.

Do you find this difficult to conceive? Living on land as most of us do, it may seem so. But we should not forget that, in its present state, 71 percent of the earth's surface is covered by water. Only 29 percent is land surface. Also, did you realize that, while the average height of the land surface is only one-half mile above sea level, the average depth of all the oceans is two and a half miles? Earth is truly a watery planet. In fact, *The Sea,* a Life Nature Library publication (Danish edition), says:

> "If all the irregularities on the earth's surface were to be smoothed out, both above and below the water, so that there were no dents or holes anywhere, no land would show at all. The ocean would cover the entire globe to a depth of 8,000 feet."

Is it possible that the earth's surface was at one time smoother or more regular than at present? Is it possible that high mountain ranges, such as the five-mile-high Himalayas, the Alps, the Andes, and the Rocky Mountains, were not always so high? Yes, it is.

The magazine *The Scientific Monthly,* for example, expresses the belief that in earth's earlier days "there were no high moun-

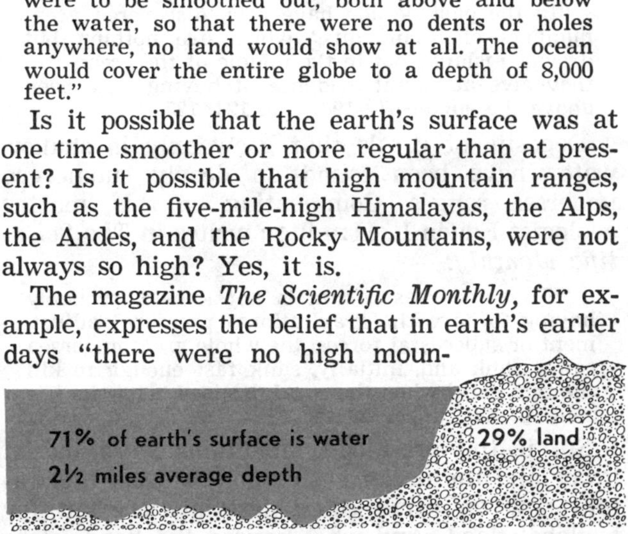

71% of earth's surface is water
2½ miles average depth
29% land

'If earth's surface were smoothed out, water would cover the entire globe to a depth of 8,000 feet'

tains forming physical or climatic barriers."[14] Abundant evidence can be found of marked changes in the earth's surface. Even in recent times sharp adjustments of land levels have taken place. As an example, in 1950 a powerful earthquake in the region of Assam, India, changed the form of entire mountain chains in the eastern Himalayas. So, when the Bible says that the floodwaters covered the highest mountains, we are not to think of water sufficient to cover Mount Everest today.

What about the ocean depths? May they also have undergone changes? There is evidence that they have. For example, the book *The Genesis Flood* says:

> "In the past decade have been discovered great numbers of 'seamounts,' which are nothing but drowned islands out in the middle of the ocean. . . . they give abundant evidence of having once been above the surface."—1967, pp. 124, 125.

Deposits of corals that grow only in shallow water have been found on deeply submerged undersea ranges. Commenting on this, marine geologist Edwin L. Hamilton writes in *The Scientific Monthly:*

> "For some reason that is not known, probably having to do with [gravitational pressure] adjustment or subcrustal forces, the whole great undersea range sank and, initially, sank fast enough to kill the reef coral when the coral dropped below its life zone in the upper waters."[15]

So, if the pre-Flood mountains were indeed lower and the ocean basins not as deep, the waters now on earth could certainly account for a global flood. And what caused the floodwaters thereafter to 'progressively recede' as the Genesis account relates? A deepening or sinking of the ocean floors, along with a rising of the land surfaces, evidently had that effect.—Compare Psalm 104:6-8.

A CHANGE IN CLIMATE

Since a globe-encircling water canopy would have caused a hothouse state reaching even to the polar regions, the falling of this water in an earth-wide flood should have produced a drastic change in earth's climate. Is there any evidence that there has been such a drastic change? Yes, there is. And the change is so striking that, without the Bible, geologists find themselves very hard pressed to explain it.

Various scientific publications present evidence that there was once an earth-wide warm climate. As an example, French scholar Henri Decugis, in *The Degeneration of the Living World,* says:

> "[The earth once] enjoyed a uniformly warm and wet climate in every latitude. . . . Islands and continents were covered with a prodigious luxuriant vegetation of continuous growth. . . . There was, at the beginning, but a slight difference in the temperatures of summer and winter. Fig-trees have been unearthed in Greenland in latitude 70° North and palms in Siberia."—1941, pp. 12, 13.

So there is evidence of what we might expect would result from the falling of a water canopy in a global flood—a drastic change in climate.

VAST, SUDDEN DESTRUCTION

Besides a change in climate, we would also naturally expect the Flood to produce earth-wide evidence of a vast, sudden destruction. Is there such evidence? Yes, and it is found, not in just one locality, but throughout the earth.

Excavations have uncovered the bones and carcasses of countless thousands of animals buried together. These are often from animals that would not normally herd together. The circumstances in which they are found indicate that they were all killed at the same time and then swept together by a gigantic force.

Concerning such excavations in Alaska, Professor F. C. Hibben states:

> "There is evidence of atmospheric disturbances of unparalleled violence. Mammoth and bison alike were torn and twisted as though by a cosmic hand in Godly rage. . . . The animals were simply torn apart and scattered over the landscape like things of straw and string, even though some of them weighed several tons."[16]

French writer François Derrey refers to this in his book *La Terre Cette Inconnue* and adds:

> "The pits of Alaska are not unique. All over the world there have been found charnel houses of this nature, piled high with the broken remains of thousands of animals."

Even more amazing is the fact that carcasses of tens of thousands of animals unearthed in the extremely cold north are of types that do not normally live in cold regions. Some were frozen solid and so well preserved that the flesh, when thawed after thousands of years, could be eaten. Green grass and flowers, fully preserved, have been found in such animals' stomachs and between their teeth. Even fruit trees were discovered in these locations, the leaves and fruit perfectly preserved by sudden freezing. It is plain that these trees were growing and the animals were grazing in a warm climate when a sudden catastrophe struck.

The evidence is just what one would expect to result from the fall of a vast insulating moisture blanket. The polar regions were suddenly plunged into a deep freeze. Animals in or near those regions were trapped and frozen solid. Creatures overtaken elsewhere were buried in great numbers under earth and debris. Neither natural death, nor drowning by ordinary means, nor death by disease can satisfactorily explain all this evidence. But an earth-wide flood accompanied by a drastic change in climate can.

UNIVERSAL FLOOD TRADITIONS

We would expect that the gigantic catastrophe of an earth-wide flood would be long remembered by mankind. Other than the Bible record, is there any evidence that this was so?

Yes, in all parts of the earth there are people with traditions of a great flood, one that drowned all but a select few. As the book *Target: Earth* states:

> "In the ordinary experience of man floods are not of such great or of such wide spread occurrence that he would generate a story of an overwhelming, all-exterminating flood. . . . Why then should practically all races of men have this legend of a great deluge? Why should people who lived far from the ocean in dry highland country such as central Mexico or central Asia have a legend of a flood? . . .
>
> "If universal deluge had not been an actuality, then some races would have had their wicked ancestors being eliminated by awesome volcanic eruptions, great blizzards, drought, . . . Thus the universality of the deluge story is one of the best arguments for its truth.
>
> "Any of these legends, taken by itself, might be brushed aside as the working of a vivid human imagination, but . . . taken together, from the world-wide aspect, . . . they become well-nigh incontrovertible."—1953, pp. 239, 253.

COULD THE ARK HAVE HELD ALL THOSE ANIMALS?

Since the Bible says that Noah brought some of all the various kinds of land animals and flying creatures into the ark, some persons have asked, "How could there possibly have been room for all those animals?"

According to the Bible's description, the ark was a great floating chest or box, having no prow or stern. It did not need these, for it was designed only to float on top of the water. Its size was 300 cubits long, 50 cubits wide and 30 cubits high. A cubit is estimated as from 17.5 to 24 inches long. On the basis of the lower figure, the ark would have been 437 feet 6 inches long, 72 feet 11 inches wide and 43 feet 9 inches high. Only in recent years have ships been built larger. The ark had lower, second and third stories. —Genesis 6:14-16.

If we allow 100,000 cubic feet of space for deck floors and other inside parts, there still remain nearly 1,300,000 cubic feet of usable space. This is equal to the carrying capacity of ten freight trains of about forty-eight American stockcars each!

Also, investigation reveals that, of some 3,000 "species" of land mammals classified by zoologists, only about 300 include any that are larger than a horse, whereas some 2,200 are no larger than a rabbit.[17] Marine mammals such as the huge whales and dolphins would be no problem, as they would have remained outside the ark. So Noah had relatively few large animals to care for.

Another key factor to keep in mind is that the present classification scientists call "species"

Not all varieties of animals needed to be in the ark. All interfertile types of the dog family, for example, could have come from just one pair.

is not the same as the Bible "kinds" that Noah took into the ark. (Genesis 6:20) For example, there are many "species" in the cat family, such as tigers, panthers, leopards, and so forth. But many of these could have descended from an original cat "kind." So, too, with the various types of dogs in the dog family. Thus, not all of today's animal varieties needed to be in the ark. Only representative numbers of each "kind" would be required. When the facts are analyzed, it becomes plain that the ark's capacity was sufficient to hold them all.

THE CHRISTIAN VIEWPOINT

There are, of course, those who doubt the account of the global flood. Strangely enough, among them are some professed Christian religious organizations. For example, the latest Lutheran and Catholic encyclopedias say the Flood account was based on 'myth' or 'imagination.'[18] But in view of all the evidence presented, is there any sound basis for objecting to this Bible account? Every point has been shown to be both reasonable and in accord with known facts.

Those who reject the account put themselves not only at odds with the actual evidence but also in conflict with Jesus Christ, the Founder of Christianity. Jesus spoke of "the days of Noah" and of the destruction of those who "took no note until the flood came and swept them all away." (Matthew 24:37-39) Jesus' apostle Paul accepted as fact the Bible's Flood account, for he wrote that Noah "constructed an ark for the saving of his household." (Hebrews 11:7) The apostle Peter said that God "kept Noah, a preacher of righteousness, safe with seven others when he brought a deluge upon a world of ungodly people."—2 Peter 2:5.

Is it wise to reject the Bible account of the Flood as nothing more than a myth, or to brush it aside as of little consequence? Is it being honest with oneself?

This is a point for serious consideration. Why? Because the Bible points to the Flood as a warning example of a greater destruction that is to come from God upon those who do not heed his Word, and it strongly warns that such destruction is due to come upon the generation now living on the earth. (Matthew 24:36-42; 2 Peter 3:5-7) If this warning truly is from God, will your attitude toward the Bible and your course of life cause you to be looked upon with favor when that day of accounting arrives?

CHAPTER 4

The Bible and Ancient History —Do They Agree?

THE book that is to measure up as the Word of God must contain the truth no matter what subject it discusses. When it mentions a certain town or place, it must have existed. When it speaks of a particular person, he must actually have lived. When it says a certain event took place, it must have happened. In its treatment of history, does the Bible show itself to be such a book?

In the last two centuries ancient history has been illuminated in marked degree by archaeological excavations. The tombs of the Pharaohs in Egypt, the magnificent palaces of the kings of Assyria, Babylon and Persia, as well as the ruins of hundreds of cities and towns, have yielded literally tons of material. What has this revealed as regards Biblical history?

NUMEROUS POINTS OF HARMONY

The geographical locations mentioned in the Bible have been found to be accurate time after time. Likely for this reason, Dr. Ze'ev Shremer, leader of a geological expedition in the Sinai Peninsula, stated:

> "We have our own maps and geodetic survey plans, of course, but where the Bible and the maps are at odds, we opt for The Book."[19]

Names of persons previously found only in the Bible have also turned up in ancient inscriptions that have been unearthed. Near the Ishtar Gate in Babylon were found a number of cuneiform tablets containing lists of food rations for workers and captives. Some of these revealed the name of "Yaukin, king of the land of Yahud," the Babylonian form of "Jehoiachin, king of Judah." The Bible account at 2 Kings 25:27-30 describes the Babylonian captivity of Jehoiachin and his being given a daily food allowance. Other kings of Judah and Israel, such as Ahaz, Manasseh, Omri, Jehu, Menahem and Hoshea, all appear on cuneiform records of ancient Assyrian emperors.

Besides these Hebrew kings, many other historical names mentioned in the Bible but previously missing from non-Biblical histories have come to light. For centuries the Bible alone made mention of the Assyrian emperor Sargon. (Isaiah 20:1) Then in 1843 the immense ruins of his palace were uncovered near Khorsabad. Today Sargon II is one of the more completely documented Assyrian kings.

Events mentioned in the Bible, also customs, titles, and other details, have often been illustrated or paralleled by inscriptions and other objects unearthed. This is true of chapters 39 to 50 of Genesis, which describe the life of Joseph in Egypt in the early part of the second millennium B.C.E. Egyptian monuments, inscriptions and paintings illustrate a remarkable number of the account's features. The Egyptian names, the prison house, the titles "chief of the cupbearers" and "chief of the bakers," the requirement of shaving when about to appear before Pharaoh, the position of prime minister and food administrator (assigned to Joseph by Pharaoh), the strong influence of magicians in the Egyptian court, the Egyptian burial practices—all are clearly paralleled by the things found. The book *New Light on Hebrew Origins* says about the writer of the account concerning Joseph:

> "He employs the correct title in use and exactly as it was used at the period referred to, and, where there is no Hebrew equivalent, he simply adopts the Egyptian word and transliterates it into Hebrew."—1936, p. 174.

The Bible account bears all the earmarks of genuine history based on eyewitness testimony.

IS THE HARMONY ABSOLUTE?

Does this mean that there is now absolute harmony between the Bible and every other ancient history? Definitely not. Nor should we think that all the archaeologists' interpretations of their findings agree in every respect with the Bible. Well, then, should this change our view of the Bible and its being genuinely historical? Not at all.

For one thing, there are many passages in the Bible that reach back to times beyond those covered by any other accepted ancient histories. Furthermore, most modern historians acknowledge that the ancient records of Egypt and Mesopotamia cease to be of value when they reach a certain point in the past. As an example, what is known as "The Sumerian King List" from Babylonia begins like this:

> "When kingship was lowered from heaven, kingship was (first) in Eridu. (In) Eridu, A-lulim (became) king and ruled 28,800 years. Alalgar ruled 36,000 years. Two kings (thus) ruled it for 64,800 years."—*Ancient Near Eastern Texts,* p. 265.

Finally, after listing eight kings as ruling for a grand total of 241,000 years, it speaks of the 'flood as sweeping over the earth.' Would there be any purpose in trying to harmonize the Bible's account of pre-Flood times with this Babylonian account? To what extent, then, can we expect harmony between the Bible and ancient history?

EARLY POST-FLOOD HISTORY

Consider the Bible's post-Flood history. It shows mankind spreading out over the earth from one central point during the latter part of the third millennium B.C.E. That central point was the Plains of Shinar. There, the Bible states, men acted contrary to God's will in proceeding to build a city called Babel and attempting to construct a great tower with its "top in the heavens." God confused their common language, and "scattered them from there over all the surface of the earth." (Genesis 11:1-9) Should we expect history or archaeology to confirm this account? If so, to what extent?

The place is known. Archaeologists have located the ancient site of the city of Babel or Babylon in Mesopotamia. But historians and archaeologists today acknowledge that they can neither prove nor disprove the rest of the account. Take the matter of the origin of different languages within the human race. Professor of Anthropology and Linguistics G. L. Trager shows that, while the evidence points to a common age of all ancient tongues, scholars do not know how they began. He says:

> "Historical knowledge about existing languages goes back only a few thousand years . . . There are no 'primitive' languages, but all languages seem to be equally old and equally developed.

"We do not know whether all languages proceed from a single original source, or how long they have been developing."[20]

However, something important is revealed in the study of the spread of ancient languages to different parts of the earth. What is that? One particular part of the earth is seen as the focal point from which the spreading began. Identifying that point, Sir Henry Rawlinson, Oriental language scholar, says:

"If we were to be guided by the mere intersection of linguistic paths, and independently of all reference to the Scriptural record, *we should still be led to fix on the plains of Shinar* [in Mesopotamia], *as the focus from which the various lines had radiated.*"[21]

Contrary to what the Bible says, historians previously pointed to Egypt in Africa as the site of the earliest civilization. However, note what archaeologist Jaquetta Hawkes, editor of *The World of the Past,* states:

"Egypt was long believed to be . . . the centre from which all civilization was carried to the rest of the world. Archaeological studies have proved otherwise. Both in the beginning of farming . . . and in the first development of true civilization, Egypt played a role secondary to that of Western Asia." —Vol. I, p. 443.

This lines up with the Biblical account.

Besides this, the Bible's statement that the builders of the "tower of Babel" used kiln-fired bricks, and bitumen for mortar, corresponds with the evidence of numerous ziggurats (or towers in the form of staged pyramids) that have been found. Bricks were the common building material, and a tower at Ur had bitumen (asphalt) as mortar. No claim is made, of course, that any of these is the original tower. However, it is interesting that inscriptions in Babylon relating to these towers even echo the same expression found in the Bible account: "Its top shall reach the heavens."—Compare Genesis 11:4.

It can be seen, then, that the ancient records, when available, harmonize with the Bible on matters of geography, customs and other details. But they are usually lacking in the more vital points, for they do not explain *why* certain conditions arose, *why* certain events took place. And it is obviously useless to expect that the non-Biblical accounts would acknowledge any intervention in human affairs by Jehovah, the God of the Bible.

EVALUATING THE ANCIENT HISTORIANS

This leads to another sound reason why we should not expect full harmony between the other ancient histories and the Bible. It involves the men who wrote those histories. As pointed out in the 1966 *World Book Encyclopedia:*

> "The historian is a human being. He loves and hates, just as other men do. He has his own beliefs, values, attitudes, opinions, hopes, and fears, . . . He selects the things he considers important." —Vol. 9, p. 233.

This raises questions: What kind of men recorded the ancient secular histories? What claim do they have to our trust and confidence? Does their background show them to be more reliable than the Bible writers?

In many ancient nations it was the custom to entrust the recording of events to the religious priesthood. Even royal scribes were apparently trained in schools run by the priesthood. The vast majority of ancient inscriptions from Egypt, Assyria, Babylon and Persia were devoted either to glorifying the king or the national gods, whom the king represented. Historians and archaeologists may choose to present these national records as "secular" in contrast to the Bible's "religious" account. But the fact is that those ancient non-Biblical records are far more religious than they are "secular." Like it or not, then, religion inescapably enters into the picture. So, one is faced with the question: Did the other ancient religions produce more honest recorders of history than did the religion of the Bible?

Consider, for example, the Assyrian scribes. On the basis of much research, Assyriologist D. D. Luckenbill says concerning their records:

> "One soon discovers that the accurate portrayal of events as they took place, year by year during the king's reign, was not the guiding motive of the royal scribes. . . . Often it is clear that royal vanity demanded playing fast and loose with historical accuracy."—*Ancient Records of Assyria and Babylonia,* Vol. I, p. 7.

Illustrating this, another authority on the ancient Middle East, Professor Olmstead, makes reference to the "cool taking by [Assyrian Emperor Ashurbanipal] of bit after bit of the last two Egyptian campaigns of his father until in the final edition there is nothing that he has not claimed for himself." (*Assyrian Historiography,* p. 7) So, accuracy and honesty were not outstanding traits of the ancient non-Hebrew scribes.

In view of these factors, what would we reasonably expect from such histories? Suppose the Bible account relates a victory by one of these nations over the kingdom of Israel or of Judah. Would the non-Biblical records be likely to record this? Most certainly! Of course, they might also exaggerate the size of their victory, for cuneiform inscriptions prove that this was their custom. On the other hand, if such a nation suffered a defeat, would their national records be likely to tell of this? Consider the following example.

EXODUS FROM EGYPT

Many persons have asked why Egyptian records are completely silent about the exodus of the nation of Israel from Egypt, and the destruction of Egypt's elite forces in the Red Sea. Here we present the answer given to that question by Egyptologist J. A. Wilson:

> "Egyptian records were always positive, emphasizing the successes of the pharaoh or the god, whereas failures and defeats were never mentioned, except in some context of the distant past."[22]

New Egyptian dynasties might even erase from the earlier records anything considered undesirable. For instance, it appears that after the death of Queen Hatshepsut, Thutmose III had her name and figure chiseled out of a stone monument discovered at Deir el-Bahri, Egypt.

But really, is that so different from our own time? Do political governments today willingly tell their people all about their major defeats and failures? Or, to the extent possible, do they try to cover them over? And is it unheard of for them to erase from their history books anything favorable to a hated minority? Did not this happen in Germany under the Nazi regime? Have not other governments had their nation's history books rewritten for political or other reasons?

No wonder, then, that the names of Moses, Aaron and other Israelites, as well as the events connected with them, are missing from ancient Egyptian records. It would be most unusual if

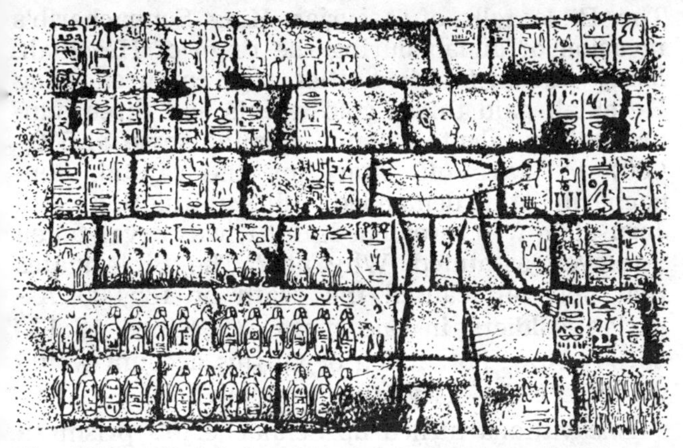

The Bible tells of Judah's defeat by Pharaoh Shishak; on this temple wall at Karnak that Egyptian victory is recorded. But why do Egyptian inscriptions say nothing of Israel's exodus from Egypt? Would you expect them to commemorate a defeat?

they were there! For Egyptian history to record those events would, in effect, have been admitting what Exodus 12:12 says, that 'Jehovah executed judgment on all the gods of Egypt.'

By contrast, consider the Bible account of Pharaoh Shishak's successful invasion of the land of unfaithful Judah during the reign of Solomon's son Rehoboam. (1 Kings 14:25, 26) Now we find Egyptian confirmation! Shishak proudly recorded his victory in Palestine on the temple walls of Karnak in Egypt. Among the towns he claimed to have captured are Gibeon and Socoh of the kingdom of Judah.

COMPARING OTHER ANCIENT RECORDS

Were other ancient histories like those of Egypt? Consider a case from Assyrian history.

The Bible tells of Assyrian King Sennacherib's invasion of Judah during the reign of Hezekiah. Many Judean fortified cities were captured. King Hezekiah paid thirty gold talents and three hundred silver talents (a sum equaling some $1,500,000) to stave off attack on the capital. Sennacherib still demanded full capitulation, and Jerusalem was threatened. But it was never taken nor even assaulted. Why not? The Bible states that Jehovah caused the death of 185,000 Assyrian soldiers in one night. (2 Kings 18:13–19:36) Now, how much of all this account would we expect the Assyrians to record?

Excavations turned up Sennacherib's prism (a many-sided clay cylinder) containing the Assyrian account of this invasion of Judah. What did it say? In part we read:

> "As to Hezekiah, the Jew, he did not submit to my [Sennacherib's] yoke, I laid siege to 46 of his strong cities, walled forts and to the countless small villages in their vicinity, and conquered (them) . . . I drove out (of them) 200,150 people . . . [as] booty. [Hezekiah] I made a prisoner in Jerusalem, his royal residence, like a bird in a cage . . . Hezekiah himself . . . did send me, later, to Nineveh, my lordly city, together with 30 talents of gold, 800 talents of silver, . . . all kinds of valuable treasures, . . . In order to deliver the tribute and to do obeisance as a slave he sent his (personal) messenger."[23]

So, Sennacherib's version coincides with the Bible where Assyrian victories are concerned. He inflates the number of silver talents exacted by 500—something to be expected—and speaks of a huge number of captives. Giving his estimation of Assyrian honesty in such matters, Professor Olmstead says:

" . . . when Sennacherib tells us that he took from . . . Judah no less than 200,150 prisoners, and that in spite of the fact that Jerusalem itself was not captured, we may deduct the 200,000 as a product of the exuberant fancy of the Assyrian scribe and accept the 150 as somewhere near the actual number captured and carried off."—*Assyrian Historiography,* pp. 7, 8.

Note that Sennacherib gives no explanation as to why he did not capture Jerusalem. He even goes so far as to claim that he trustingly left for Assyria with only a 'promise to pay' on Hezekiah's part. Professor Emeritus of Semitic Languages, Ira M. Price, plainly states:

"This order of events looks like a screen to cover up something which he does not wish to mention."[24]

Of the wholesale loss of troops—nothing. Should we expect it? Professor Jack Finegan comments in his book *Light from the Ancient Past:*

"In view of the general note of boasting which pervades the inscriptions of the Assyrian kings, . . . it is hardly to be expected that Sennacherib would record such a defeat."—1946, p. 178.

And again we may ask, Is this so different from today?

When it came to honest reporting, the Babylonians and Persians differed little from the ancient Egyptians and Assyrians. Consider just one example: the "Persian Verse Account of Nabonidus." Described by Assyriologist A. Leo Oppenheim as forming, along with the "Cyrus Cylinder," a "distorted report of the entire reign of Nabonidus," and called by Professor Olmstead "deliberate propaganda," it nevertheless reveals what was done to Babylonian historical records after Cyrus conquered Babylon. The restored text reads:

> " . . . [Nabonidus'] picture/symbol he [Cyrus] effaced, . . . the inscriptions of his name are erased, [. . . whatever he (Nabonidus) had cre]ated, he (Cyrus) let fire burn up."[25]

Should we expect, then, that Babylonian records would be complete?

And since this practice existed, should we be surprised if the names of persons mentioned in the Bible, such as Daniel, his three Hebrew companions, or that of the Jewess Esther, who became queen of Persia, are missing from ancient national histories? Remember, these histories were usually compiled and kept by priestly scribes, many of whom vigorously opposed the religion of the Jews. So, it would be strange indeed if the names and deeds of the Jews were commemorated or allowed to remain. Or, for that matter, even the names of certain kings who showed them favor, such as Darius the Mede.—Daniel 6:1-28.

DIFFERENCES NO CAUSE FOR CONCERN

Should we, then, become disturbed because certain features of the Bible record are not found in other histories, or because details appear to differ? Not at all. The two examples that follow —involving Sennacherib and Belshazzar—show why we should never underestimate the Bible's truthfulness.

At 2 Kings 19:36, 37 the Bible tells of the assassination of Assyrian King Sennacherib by two of his sons, Adrammelech and Sharezer. Yet both the account attributed to Babylonian King Nabonidus and that presented by Babylonian priest Berossus (of the third century B.C.E.) mention only one son as involved in the slaying. Should this disturb us? No. They may have mentioned only one son because of his taking the lead in the plot, or for some similar reason. Be that as it may, the accuracy of the Bible account has been borne out by the discovery of a fragmentary prism of Esar-haddon, a third son mentioned in the Bible as succeeding to Sennacherib's throne. It says:

> "A firm determination fell upon my brothers. They . . . turned to their deeds of violence, . . . To gain the kingship they slew Sennacherib their father."[26]

Thus, the Bible simply gave a more complete picture than the other previously known sources.

A similar case in point is that of Belshazzar. The book of Daniel presents Belshazzar as king of Babylon at the time of its fall. Other ancient sources, such as the Babylonian Berossus and the Greek historians Herodotus and Xenophon, mention only Nabonidus as Babylon's king at that time. Recently, however, cuneiform tablets have turned up to show that Belshazzar was Nabonidus' son, that he served as coregent for several years, and that, in his father's absence, he was ruling over Babylon at the time of its fall. It is evidently for this reason that Belshazzar offered to make Daniel the "third ruler in the kingdom," rather than the second, since second was Belshazzar's own position. (Daniel 5:16, 29) While the histories of Berossus, Herodotus and Xenophon may simply have omitted these points, Yale Professor R. P. Dougherty, comparing the book of Daniel with those histories, voices the opinion:

> "The Scriptural account may be interpreted as excelling because it employs the name Belshazzar, because it attributes royal power to Belshazzar,

and because it recognizes that a dual rulership existed in the kingdom."—*Nabonidus and Belshazzar*, p. 200.

Many cases could be cited, but these two are sufficient to show that an apparent lack of harmony is often merely an improper interpretation of matters. They illustrate that it is unwise to make an issue out of a superficial difference, attempting to pit the non-Biblical accounts against the Bible record.

DATING EVENTS IN HISTORY

In view of the evidence, when a difference appears between the Bible date for an event and a date advanced by historians on the basis of pagan histories and the interpretation of archaeologists, which should have greater claim to our confidence?

In its chapter "The Science of Historical Dating" the book *The Secret of the Hittites* makes this observation:

> "Anyone approaching the study of ancient history for the first time must be impressed by the positive way modern historians date events which took place thousands of years ago. In the course of further study this wonder will, if anything, increase. For as we examine the sources of ancient history we see how scanty, inaccurate, or downright false, the records were even at the time they were first written. And poor as they originally were, they are poorer still as they have come down to us: half destroyed by the tooth of time or by the carelessness and rough usage of men."—P. 134.

The book then goes on to describe the historian's framework of chronology as a "purely hypothetical structure, and one which threatens to come apart at every joint." Well illustrating this is the variety of dates offered by different historians for the start of Egypt's first dynasty. They range all the way from 5867 B.C.E. to 2224 B.C.E.!

The chronological history of the ancient non-Hebrew nations as it stands today is a patchwork. It has been laboriously pieced together from bits of information obtained from widely scattered sources. The Bible, by contrast, consolidates within its pages an unusually coherent and detailed history stretching through some four thousand years, including a graphic and true-to-life record of events in the nation of Israel from its birth onward for a period of nearly sixteen centuries. This gives a stability to Bible chronology that other ancient histories do not have.

THE BIBLE'S CLAIM TO OUR CONFIDENCE

What reasons do we have, then, for placing superior confidence in the Bible record as historically accurate? Why should we believe that the men used to write the Bible were more honest than the scribes of other ancient nations?

The evidence is found within the Bible itself. And the contrast between the content of the Biblical accounts and the other ancient records is, beyond denial, enormous. The non-Biblical records are in nothing more notable than for their boasting, their glorification of individuals, their materialistic outlook—all of which reflect their religious views. Notably lacking are candor, modesty and humility—the very factors that distinguish the Bible from all other ancient histories. Read these words from an inscription of Assyrian King Esar-haddon:

> "I am powerful, I am all powerful. I am a hero, I am gigantic, I am colossal."[27]

Compare them with these words of Judean King Jehoshaphat at 2 Chronicles 20:6, 12:

> "O Jehovah the God of our forefathers, are you not God in the heavens, and are you not dominating over all the kingdoms of the nations, and are there not in your hand power and mightiness, with no one to hold his ground against you? . . . For in us there is no power before this large crowd that is coming against us; and we ourselves do not know what we ought to do, but our eyes are toward you."

Do you not agree that there is a vast difference between them? Only in the Bible record do we find such frank admission of human frailties, the record of disgraceful calamity caused by unfaithful Israelite kings and of the humiliation of captivity and oppression.—Psalm 51:1-5; Nehemiah 1:5-7.

The whole message of the Bible is that the worship of the true God brings blessings in the form of peace, righteousness, justice and contentment, both now and in the eternal future, whereas the violation of God's laws and counsel brings grief, delinquency, strife and death. The true-to-life candor of the historical accounts illustrating this message argues strongly for the validity of the message itself.

When weighing the Bible record against the other ancient histories, remember this: Those non-Biblical accounts may be engraved in stone or inscribed in clay—solid materials that have endured for millenniums. But the ambitious men and empires of whom they wrote and the many gods whose worship they expounded have no effect on people's lives today. They are dead museum pieces, and the message about them is a dead message. The Bible records were evidently written on papyrus or vellum, which soon perished due to continued use and the effects of time and weather. But their message is alive! They have been copied and recopied, read and reread, continuously from generation to generation for thousands of years. And though the religions of the ancient Egyptians, Assyrians and others have died, the worship of Jehovah, the God of the Bible, is the moving force, to this day, in the lives of hundreds of thousands of persons in all the earth.—Compare Isaiah 40:6-8.

The discovery of ancient non-Biblical histories has often demonstrated the rightness of the Bible record in the face of criticism. Those histories revealed numerous names of persons, peoples and places, and described customs and events, previously known only in the Bible record. But we cannot reasonably expect the inscriptions left by imperfect, power-hungry men to harmonize completely with the Bible. Nor can we hope to find confirmation of Jehovah's past dealings with his servants by searching the writings prepared by worshipers of the numerous mythical gods and goddesses of the past. Such ancient records have no real claim to our confidence. On the other hand, is it not encouraging and refreshing to find in the Bible record the satisfying ring of truth that you would expect from the Word of God?

CHAPTER 5

Early Christianity —Is the Record Sound?

THE Bible record is climaxed by its account of early Christianity. Written in Greek in the first century of our Common Era, this account relates the teachings and the powerful works attributed to Jesus Christ and his apostles. In its pages, Jesus is quoted as saying that he spoke 'the truth that he heard from God.' (John 8:40) And the apostle Paul reports that believers accepted its message, "not as the word of men, but, just as it truthfully is, as the word of God." —1 Thessalonians 2:13.

But do the facts warrant such confidence in the Bible's record of early Christianity? Is it factual, or does it simply set out the imaginative writings of religious men?

Of interest in this connection is the comparison made by Orientalist George Rawlinson, who writes:

> "Christianity . . . is in nothing more distinguished from the other religions of the world than in its objective or historical character. The religions of Greece and Rome, of Egypt, India, Persia, and the East generally, were speculative systems, which did not even seriously postulate an historical basis. . . . it is otherwise with the religion of the Bible."

But, if this is true of the historical aspects of

the record, what does it indicate as to the teachings themselves? Rawlinson continues:

> "Whether we look to the Old or the New Testament, . . . we find a scheme of doctrine which is bound up with facts; which depends absolutely upon them; which is null and void without them; and which may be regarded as for all practical purposes established if they are shown to deserve acceptance."[28]

We have already examined the evidence in connection with the Hebrew Scriptures, referred to by many as the "Old Testament," and found these to be sound. Do the facts indicate the same reliability for the Christian Greek Scriptures, or "New Testament"?

JESUS A HISTORICAL PERSON

Let us turn our attention first to Jesus Christ himself. Is it a historical fact that he lived in Palestine during the early part of our Common Era?

Tacitus, a Roman historian who lived during the latter part of the first century C.E., was no Christian. But in his *Annals* he stated this as fact:

> "Christus [Latin for "Christ"], from whom the name [Christian] had its origin, suffered the extreme penalty during the reign of Tiberius at the hands of one of our procurators, Pontius Pilatus [Pilate]."[29]

Josephus, who was not a Christian but a Jewish historian in the first century, also makes mention of Jesus Christ. In his *Antiquities of the Jews,* Josephus tells of the execution of James whom he refers to as "the brother of Jesus, who was called Christ."—Book XX, chap. IX, par. 1.

With good reason, then, Dr. T. R. Glover, lecturer in ancient history at Cambridge University, says:

"If the ordinary canons of history, used in every other case, hold good in this case, Jesus is undoubtedly an historical person. If he is not an historical person, the only alternative is that there is no such thing as history at all—it is delirium, nothing else; and a rational being would be better employed in the collection of snuff-boxes. And if history is impossible, so is all other knowledge."[30]

ARE THE GOSPEL ACCOUNTS WORTHY OF ACCEPTANCE?

Though acknowledging that Jesus Christ actually did live, some still ask how we can be sure that the accounts of his life as set out in the four Gospels are accurate. Did Jesus really do the things recorded in the Bible?

There were no motion pictures or tape recorders in those days. No one is walking the earth today who lived then. So, we must obviously rely on the written testimony of persons who lived at that time. Where is such testimony available? The only detailed accounts in existence are in the Bible itself. Interestingly, within its pages are four Gospels, four distinct accounts, all harmonizing, yet each one written from a different viewpoint and each one providing certain details that the others do not.

But what of the testimony from other sources? Consider the accounts in the Jewish Talmud. It is true that these clash with the Gospels, but notice how. The conflict centers on the *means* by which certain events recorded in the Gospels took place, not the reality of the events themselves. Thus the Talmud does not question that Jesus was born, but only the miraculous nature of his birth. It does not deny that he performed healing and other wonderful works, but claims that they were done by magic and sorcery. It attacks nothing else in the Gospel accounts. Does this disprove the Gospels? Not at all. The Gospel accounts themselves show that these were among the very matters on which Jesus' religious opposers contended with him. (John 8:41, 48; Matthew 12:24) So, unintentionally, the Talmud supports the Gospel record.

After examining the Talmudic references to Jesus, Jewish scholar Klausner impartially acknowledged:

> "Nothing in the Gospels was denied: it was only perverted into a source of ridicule and blame." —*Jesus of Nazareth*, pp. 18, 19, 53.

The ancient Roman writers also make mention of Christianity, though most of them do so only briefly. Tacitus, Suetonius, Juvenal, and even Nero's tutor Seneca confirm that Christianity quickly spread to all parts of the Roman Empire.

But it is hardly to be expected that these worshipers of mythical gods would speak out in favor of the message contained in the Christian Scriptures. After all, those Scriptures attacked the very foundation of their polytheistic worship. So it comes as no surprise that Celsus, a sharp-witted philosopher of the second century C.E., wrote a severe attack on Christianity. His statements were quoted in detail by Origen, a prominent church leader of the next century who refuted them. In his lengthy argument, Celsus condemns, rejects and ridicules the Gospel accounts. But nowhere does he produce any historical evidence to support his accusations.

Typical of his work are his arguments that Christ could not have had a divine origin since the Gospel accounts show him as of humble origin, materially poor, as being betrayed, suffering and being put to death. (Origen, *Against Celsus,* Books I, II) Here it is readily apparent that, while Celsus accepts what the Bible says about the earthly circumstances of Christ, he takes issue with what it says about Christ's origin simply on the basis of a personal opinion—an opinion that is the product, not of facts, but of his own religious outlook.

So what do the facts show? Is there in this non-Biblical testimony any powerful evidence that proves the Bible record of early Christianity to be untruthful? As you ponder that question, consider the contents of the Christian Greek Scriptures themselves.

STRONG INDICATIONS OF RELIABILITY

Unlike mythological writings, the Christian Greek Scriptures are built around people who actually lived and places that exist even to this day. With great care they specify the time in which the events occurred. On this matter attorney Irwin H. Linton, writing in the book *A Lawyer Examines the Bible,* says:

> "While romances, legends and false testimony are careful to place the events related in some distant place and some indefinite time, thereby violating the first rules we lawyers learn of good pleading, that 'the declaration must give time and place,' the Bible narratives give us the date and place of the things related with the utmost precision."—P. 38.

This is illustrated by the statement at Luke 3:1, 2:

> "In the fifteenth year of the reign of Tiberius Caesar, when Pontius Pilate was governor of Judea, and Herod was district ruler of Galilee, but Philip his brother was district ruler of the country of Ituraea and Trachonitis, and Lysanias was district

ruler of Abilene, in the days of chief priest Annas and of Caiaphas, God's declaration came to John the son of Zechariah in the wilderness."

Seven separate political and religious officials are here named along with their titles. For Luke's account to be correct, all of these had to be living and occupying the specified offices at one and the same time, and in the regions stated. They *were*. And you can prove that for yourself by consulting history books. Luke obviously was making no idle boast when he wrote at the beginning of the Gospel bearing his name: "I have traced all things from the start with accuracy . . . that you may know fully the certainty of the things that you have been taught."—Luke 1:3, 4.

The accuracy of the Christian Greek Scriptures is likewise made evident in the book of Acts. As F. F. Bruce of the University of Manchester states:

"[The writer of Acts] sets his narrative in the framework of contemporary history; his pages are full of references to city magistrates, provincial governors, client kings, and the like, and these references time after time prove to be just right for the place and time in question. With a minimum of words he conveys the true local colour of the widely differing cities mentioned in his story. And his description of Paul's voyage to Rome . . . remains to this day one of our most important documents of ancient seamanship."[31]

At one time critics objected to certain aspects of this Bible record. They did not believe that the Bible's use of the Greek word *politar'khes* was correct in reference to the "city rulers" of Thessalonica. Did the Bible prove unreliable? To the contrary, some nineteen ancient inscriptions have since been found that agree with the Bible's use of this previously unknown title. And five of these were from Thessalonica.—Acts 17:6, 8.

The book of Acts was also belittled by critics for calling Sergius Paulus, the governor of Cyprus, a "proconsul." (Acts 13:7) But the criticism was unfounded and, in fact, was silenced when an ancient inscription was unearthed on that island bearing the words "proconsul Paulus."

Dozens of similar examples could be cited. However, when evaluating the truthfulness of writings there is another question we should ask: Do the writers seek to exalt themselves? For humility and honesty usually go hand in hand.

How do the Christian Greek Scriptures measure up in this respect? In a very frank manner the writers expose their own weaknesses and failings. They tell us that they were looked down upon by the religious leaders as "unlettered and ordinary." (Acts 4:13) They honestly admit that they were slow to understand, had often been of "little faith" and had been reproved for disputing over their personal importance. (Matthew 16:5-12; 17:18-20; Luke 22:24-27) They admit that they all abandoned Jesus at the time of his arrest, Peter even denying three times any association with Jesus. (Matthew 26:36-45, 56, 75) They acknowledge that they were slow to accept the initial testimony of Jesus' resurrection. (Luke 24:10, 11) Is it characteristic of men who would falsify an account to include such things? Why not portray themselves as heroes?

Similarly the letters of the apostles acknowledge that there were imperfections among the early Christians, that some slipped back into immorality, some turned apostate or materialistic, and some congregations experienced dissensions. (1 Corinthians 1:10-13; 2 Timothy 2:16-18; 4:10; 2 Peter 2:14, 17, 18, 20-22; 3 John 9) They did not try to gloss over or "whitewash" these matters. They set forth the plain facts.

It was this very candor of the Bible writers that confused Celsus. His mind, influenced

Humility and honesty mark the Bible record of early Christianity. The writers freely admit even their own shortcomings—for example, that they abandoned Jesus at the time of his arrest.

by Roman mythology, could not comprehend how the disciples could present "their Lord" in such a straightforward manner. They showed the humble circumstances of Jesus' birth and early life. They told not only of the times when Jesus was accepted by those who heard him but also of the times when he was rejected. They freely related that as a man he experienced the human feelings of thirst, hunger, tiredness and grief, and that he wept and called for help from God.

It is in these Scriptures, bearing as they do the stamp of reliable history and having an unmistakable ring of honesty, that the life of Christ is related. Do you believe that they are what they profess to be—the authentic Word of God? All the evidence points strongly in that direction.

WHY SOME REJECT THE CHRISTIAN RECORDS

Why, then, do some deny the authenticity of the Bible record of early Christianity? Why is it that increasing numbers of clergymen do so? An Anglican priest, for example, termed the Gospel accounts a "clever fabrication." And the Dean of Holmen (Church of the Royal Dockyard in Copenhagen, Denmark) is quoted in the *Kalundborg Folkeblad* as saying: "Neither is the New Testament historical. Neither is it true." As we have seen, the facts certainly do not support these charges. Why, then, are they made?

Might it be that the religions that these men represent are at odds with the high standards of the Bible? In this connection, consider this report on a statement by Austrian Cardinal Koenig from *La Stampa* of Italy on November 15, 1964:

> "Too many times professed Christianity is not the religion of Christ. Selfishness, nationalism,

colonialism, Cardinal Koenig said, have caused great calamities in history by making use of corrupt Christianity. . . .

"Gandhi [of India] used to say that European Christianity is the negation of the religion of Jesus."

What about the clergy themselves? Might their belittling of the Bible be because their own way of life is not in harmony with the Scriptures? For example, Jesus warned against putting on a display of self-righteousness before men. (Matthew 6:1-8; Luke 16:14, 15) He told his disciples that none of them should be set apart from the rest by such titles as Rabbi or Father. (Matthew 23:6-12) He taught that those taking the lead were not to "lord it over" the others but were to serve them. (Matthew 20:25-28) Rather than tell his apostles that they should take up a collection when they preached, he said: "You received free, give free." (Matthew 10:8) Could it be that the clergy do not want others to read this counsel from the Bible and be convinced of its truthfulness?

A variety of books and articles have been written in our day challenging the Christian Greek Scriptures. But what do they contain? Typically, they set out long and intricate arguments, numerous charges and insinuations. But it is all mere theorizing, the figments of the imaginations of the men who have written them. They produce no sound evidence, no historical facts, nor do they agree among themselves. Are they any different from those who opposed Jesus at the time of his trial? Mark 14:55, 56 states:

"Meantime the chief priests and the whole Sanhedrin were looking for testimony against Jesus . . . but they were not finding any. Many, indeed, were giving false witness against him, but their testimonies were not in agreement."

WHAT ACCEPTANCE OF THIS RECORD MEANS

For some people, the price of accepting what the Christian Greek Scriptures teach seems too high. It means setting aside worldly prestige and humbling themselves to become servants of God and of their fellowmen. It means adopting a new moral code. They say they cannot believe. Really, where does the problem lie? Is it that these Scriptures do not appeal to an intelligent mind, that they are lacking in evidence of reliability? Or, is it, rather, that they find acceptance only in humble hearts, those that love truth and righteousness?

In determining what attitude one will have toward the Bible account of early Christianity, it is wise to differentiate what the Bible itself says from what some religious organizations say it teaches. Accepting the Christian Greek Scriptures does not mean that one must believe that Jesus Christ was 'God on earth,' a 'God-man.' To the contrary, the apostle John wrote toward the close of his Gospel account:

> "These have been written down that you may believe that Jesus is the Christ the *Son* of God, and that, because of believing, you may have life by means of his name."—John 20:31.

Jesus never pretended to be God, but said: "The Father is greater than I am."—John 14:28.

On the other hand, can acceptance mean believing that Jesus was simply a "good man," a great "humanitarian," but otherwise no different from other men? This is the view now held by many clergymen. But it is not the teaching of the Bible.

The Bible teaches that Jesus had a prehuman existence in the spirit realm, in the presence of God, and that he willingly submitted to God's transferring his life force to earth, where he was born as a perfect human. When he was here on earth God actually spoke from the heavens, saying: "This is my Son." (John 6:62; Luke 1: 26-32; Matthew 3:17) The Bible states that Jesus was sent to minister to suffering mankind and to give his life to make possible deliverance from sickness and death. It tells us that, following Jesus' death, his heavenly Father restored him to spirit life. (John 3:16; Matthew 20:28; 1 Peter 3:18) There in the heavens, the Bible points out, Christ now rules as king; by means of him God will soon bring enduring peace, health, happiness and the opportunity for eternal life to those who exercise faith in him. (1 Corinthians 15:24-26; Revelation 21:3, 4) Acceptance of the Christian Greek Scriptures means believing these things.

If the hope here described is true, then you should want to make it your very own. It is admittedly a hope that far surpasses anything that men, with all their political, medical and technological science, can offer. Why not learn about it? Read the Christian Greek Scriptures for yourself and find out what they say is required to win God's approval and the blessings that he provides through Jesus Christ.

To believe it will require faith, it is true. But, after reviewing the evidence, is there really any sound reason for not believing?

CHAPTER 6

Are the Miracles of the Bible True?

MANY sincere persons who read the Bible find it difficult to understand how the miracles it records could really have taken place.

For example, when they read that in Joshua's time the sun stood still, they find it hard to believe. And when they read that Jesus was born of a virgin, walked on water, healed the sick and raised the dead, they realize that these events differ from their own experiences in life.

But does our not having seen such things take place prove they could not have occurred? Consider this: In recent years, have not humans, no different from yourself, performed feats that your great-grandparents would have called "impossible"? Yes, you have seen amazing things take place. However, do these scientific feats supply the reason for accepting the Bible miracles?

No, because these human achievements came through much experimenting, applying already existing physical laws and using elaborate equipment. But the miracles in the Bible are different. In fact, a miracle is usually defined as a physical act or effect that goes *beyond* all known or natural powers and that is therefore attributed to a supernatural agency. So, the surprising accomplishments of men do not explain the Bible miracles. But they do illustrate an important truth: *There is need for caution in saying that a thing is "impossible."*

In that regard, note this statement by Physiology Professor John R. Brobeck of the University of Pennsylvania:

> "A scientist is no longer able to say honestly something is impossible. He can only say it is improbable. . . . One thing that needs to be added is a source of energy unknown to us in our biological and physiological sciences. In our Scriptures this source of energy is identified as the power of God."[32]

No one can rightly say, then, that belief in miracles is "unscientific." But is it reasonable?

Well, is it not evident that some power far greater than man produced the visible universe, so gigantic that it staggers human imagination? And does not life in all its complex variety on earth testify to the operation of a creative power far beyond our comprehension? The Bible identifies that power with God. As the apostle Paul wrote to persons in Rome:

> "[God's] invisible qualities are clearly seen from the world's creation onward, because they are perceived by the things made, even his eternal power and Godship, so that they are inexcusable." —Romans 1:20.

Is it reasonable, then, for any of us here on this tiny speck in the vast universe to say that no power exists that could have produced the miracles of the Bible?

CONTRARY TO "NATURE"?

Some object, however, that miracles are contrary to the laws of "nature," that is, the laws that regulate the universe and life in it. Well, could not the One who established those laws control them so as to perform a marvelous act?

To illustrate this, suppose you want to adjust your watch to some new time schedule. You simply move the hands backward or forward. You interrupt the watch's movement, yet you violate no rule for its proper use. In fact, the maker of your watch provided for just such an adjustment. Is it not logical that the Maker of the universe could do the same, as in the instance when God is said to have caused the sun to stand still (from man's viewpoint) in Joshua's time?—Joshua 10:12-14.

The Bible relates that God's servant Elisha caused an axhead to float on the water, and that Jesus walked on the sea. (2 Kings 6:5-7; John 6:16-21) Unreasonable? Some may voice that opinion. Yet on their television screens they have seen men and objects float weightlessly while on trips through "outer space." Of course, this requires the use of huge rockets and other equipment. But why should it seem incredible that the Creator of water and of the law of gravity could by his own far greater power control what he has created, and so cause an axhead to float and enable Jesus to walk on water?

THE VIRGIN BIRTH

What about the virgin birth of Jesus recorded in the Bible? Have not even so-called Christian clergymen rejected this teaching? Surprisingly, they have. For example, Dr. William Snow, a Church of England clergyman, said:

> "Could any intelligent twentieth-century man believe . . . that Jesus was born of a Virgin without the agency of a human father?

> "If everyone who didn't believe in the Virgin Birth were asked to leave the Church of England there would be an acute shortage of clergy and hardly any professors left in our theological colleges."[33]

Note that 'intelligence' and one's living in the 'twentieth century' are specified as major reasons for doubting this miracle. Is such reasoning sound? Just how much more does the twentieth-century man know about the matter than his ancestors did?

Well, what are the basic factors involved in virgin birth? Most important is life itself. How much do twentieth-century men, including scientists, know about that? The 1966 *World Book Encyclopedia* says:

> "With the dawn of science, men began to study the different kinds of . . . living things. They learned how organisms grow, what conditions they need to live, how they respond to their surroundings, and how they reproduce. . . . But they still cannot say what life itself actually is."—Vol. 12, p. 241.

Thus, intelligent twentieth-century men can no more define life than could intelligent first-century men.

In reality, to say that a human virgin birth could not take place even by the power of the Creator just because persons today have never seen it occur betrays, not intelligence, but shallow thinking. Which is greater, the development of an individual life in a living virgin? or the creation of life itself from lifeless matter? Has anyone on earth observed the creation of life? No. Yet even twentieth-century scientists admit that life must have had a beginning. They did not see it happen. They have never been able to duplicate it in their laboratories. Yet they are certain that an unseen, unrepeated beginning did take place.

So, too, with the transmission of life. Using high-powered microscopes and other equipment, men have learned much about sperm and egg cells, about chromosomes and genes, and the chemical compounds that form them. But they still do not understand why these chemicals do what they do. In this twentieth century they can still only guess and theorize how something no bigger than a pinpoint has come to have within it all the blueprints that direct the formation and organization of billions of cells of different kinds to produce a complete human child, all in nine months.

Since life itself and the marvelous power of procreation remain beyond full human comprehension, what intelligent basis does anyone have for denying that the Source of life and of procreative powers could cause a virgin to give birth? We know only the usual way for pregnancy to take place. But this is not a sound reason for doubting that the Creator of all living things could cause it to happen by another means, in this case by transferring the life force of his heavenly Son to the womb of a virgin Jewess named Mary.

WHY MIRACLES APPEAR IN THE BIBLE RECORD

Ask yourself, would the removal of miracles from the Bible give greater reason or less reason for accepting it as the Word of God? The answer must be: less. The miracles performed by Moses and the prophets, and by Jesus and his apostles, gave powerful evidence that they did, indeed, represent God. When Pharaoh of Egypt refused to heed the message brought by Moses and Aaron, the Bible account states that Jehovah God backed them up with such unusual miracles that even the magic-practicing Egyptian priests were compelled to say: "It is the finger of God!"—Exodus 8:19.

Suppose someone today were to present himself as having come from a heavenly source and as the Son of God. Would you be inclined to accept him as such if he could do nothing that other humans could not do? Or would you reasonably expect him to be able to display evidence of divine backing by doing things that are beyond human ability? The apostle Peter, facing a public audience of thousands of persons, spoke these words:

> "Jesus the Nazarene, a man publicly shown by God to you through powerful works and portents and signs that God did through him in your midst, just as you yourselves know."—Acts 2:22.

The Bible speaks of a time, under God's kingdom, when pain and death will be removed. (Isaiah 25:8; Revelation 21:1-4) Would that promise be as convincing if it were not accompanied by the testimony that Jesus and his disciples healed painful and crippling illnesses and even brought back to life those who had died? Would the testimony of the apostles that they were eyewitnesses of Jesus' own resurrection have carried the same weight among the people of their day if they had been unable to provide positive proof of divine backing, as, for example, by the miraculous gift of speaking in languages previously unknown to them?

THE REASONABLE EVIDENCE PROVIDED

"But we do not see such things today," some may say. True, but, even if we did, would this make all men believe? Will even a miracle convince a person if he does not want to believe?

The Bible reports that Jesus resurrected Lazarus from the dead after Lazarus had been dead four days! But did this make Jesus' religious opponents believe in him? The apostle John states: "They took counsel to kill him." And not only that. John continues: "The chief priests now took counsel to kill Lazarus also, because on account of him many of the Jews were . . . putting faith in Jesus." (John 11:38-44, 53; 12:10, 11) Obviously, they did not want to be convinced.

However, the Bible gives us no reason to expect such miracles now as an evidence that the Scriptures are from God. To the contrary, it specifically states that the gifts of miraculous power would cease, being no longer necessary, when the Christian congregation passed its infancy. (1 Corinthians 12:27-31; 13:8-10) But do we have sure evidence for believing that such miracles did occur?

Well, just suppose we had an original document containing the report of a full chemical analysis of the water that Jesus is reported to have changed into wine at the marriage feast in Cana of Galilee, with a second analysis of the same liquid after the change. (John 2:1-11) Would that prove that such a miracle took place? Would not our confidence in the miracle depend, rather, on the integrity of the ones who made and certified the document? The same would be true if we had a coroner's certificate of Lazarus' death and a doctor's certificate four days later stating that Lazarus was then alive. And, although today photographs and recordings are used for documentation, even these can be falsified. Our acceptance still depends upon our trust in the ones presenting them.

Really, then, the Bible contains the strongest evidence that one could reasonably expect: the written testimony of eyewitnesses. Can we trust them? Only if we read their writings and test them for the ring of truth, for evidence of sincerity, high ideals, pure motive and intelligent conviction.

Does it make sense to you that people should live on this earth in perpetual hunger, as millions do today? Then the Bible's account of Jesus' providing food for thousands may not seem important to you. Does it seem reasonable that a simple turtle may live more than 150 years, whereas the superior creation, man, despite modern medical science, must settle for half that life-span, or even less? Then the miracles of healing recorded in the Bible may hold little interest for you. And does it seem logical to you that all prospect of seeing life again should forever end at death? Then the resurrection accounts of the Bible will stir no feeling of hope within you. On the other hand, if you find these things puzzling, if it seems clear to you that something is gravely wrong with living conditions on earth today, then the accounts of those miracles may reassure you, yes, satisfy you that the Creator is both willing and able to help mankind and that he will set these matters straight. Instead of a stumbling block, the miracles of the Bible can become one of the strong evidences for you that the Bible is the Word of God.

CHAPTER 7

Does the Bible Contradict Itself?

FOR any book to win one's confidence, it must be consistent within itself. Particularly must this be true of the Bible if it is to measure up to the claim that it is the Word of God. Is it really consistent and harmonious throughout?

Some persons will answer, "No." They say that the Bible contradicts itself. Perhaps you have heard someone say that. But think back to the incident. Did the person making that claim actually open a Bible and show you an example? Usually those who say that the Bible contradicts itself make no attempt to prove it. They really know of no proof. They are simply parroting what they have heard others say.

On the other hand, there are persons who have read statements in the Bible that they did not understand. They are puzzled, perhaps sincerely believing that there are discrepancies. Can their questions be answered satisfactorily? Where does the problem lie?

SEEMING CONTRADICTIONS IN PARALLEL ACCOUNTS

Many events in the Bible are reported on in more than one account. Even within one book of the Bible a particular subject may come up for discussion more than once. Are these parallel portions always consistent?

Someone may ask: "How can it be consistent for the apostle John to state that Jesus *'did baptizing,'* and then a few verses later to report that 'Jesus himself *did no baptizing* but his disciples did'? (John 3:22; 4:2) And if Matthew is correct in saying that an *'army officer'* entreated Jesus to cure his sick manservant, why did Luke write that he sent *'older men'* to Jesus to ask him to cure his servant? (Matthew 8:5; Luke 7:3) Further, Matthew writes that *the mother* of the sons of Zebedee approached Jesus with her sons and requested: 'Give the word that these my two sons may sit down, one at your right hand and one at your left, in your kingdom.' But Mark reports that *the two sons,* James and John, made this request. (Matthew 20:20, 21; Mark 10:35-37) If these are not contradictions, then what is the explanation?"

Ask yourself, Is it not customary in everyday speech to attribute to a person a deed that he personally authorized, and for which he is responsible, although he arranges for someone else to perform it? For example, the *Encyclopædia Britannica* (1959 edition), under the heading "Agra," says of the tomb known as the Taj Mahal: "It was built by Shah Jahan for his empress." But later on in the same article we read: "The artificers engaged during the 17 years of its construction came from all parts of Asia and probably included a French goldsmith, Austin de Bordeaux."

Now, is there anything contradictory about that? Shah Jahan authorized the building work, but others did the actual labor.

So it is with those Bible accounts. Jesus did no baptizing personally, but his disciples did baptizing under his direction. The request for the healing of the army officer's servant originated with the army officer, but he sent certain older men to present that request. And in the case of the sons of Zebedee, the mother evidently acted at their suggestion or with their approval. This is supported by Matthew's report that, on hearing about the request, the other disciples became indignant, not at the mother, but at the two brothers. (Matthew 20:24) Thus, while these accounts present matters from different standpoints, would you say that there is really any contradiction?

Obviously, a reasonable approach must be taken regarding parallel accounts. In a court case, for instance, it is unlikely that two witnesses will give precisely the same description of an accident. The fact that one witness includes or omits certain details does not in itself make the testimony of another wrong. Likewise, one portion of the Bible may give details that a parallel account elsewhere in the Bible does not, and that with no contradiction. So, when there are differences, it is not wise to be hasty in concluding that they are discrepancies.

THE WRITER'S VIEWPOINT

In other cases of supposed contradictions, the difficulty is often removed when the viewpoint of the Bible writer is considered.

Moses' use of the phrase "this side of the Jordan" illustrates this. At Numbers 35:14 *"this side* of the Jordan" means east of the Jordan. Yet Joshua speaks of the territory east of the Jordan River as *"the other side* of the Jordan."

(Joshua 14:3; 17:5; 22:4) Is the conflict between the two statements real or only apparent? Well, when Moses wrote, he was in the land of Moab, east of the Jordan, which would then be to him "this side." In the latter case Joshua was in Canaan, to the west of the river, so from his viewpoint east of the Jordan was "the other side." Thus, knowing the viewpoint in each case removes any conflict.

The same principle regarding viewpoint may be applied to the several Bible accounts about Jesus' healing of blind beggars near Jericho. Reading the accounts, you will observe that Mark and Luke report the healing of one blind man, but Matthew mentions two. Inconsistent? Well, would you say that Luke's statement that "a certain blind man" was healed conflicts with Mark's report that "Bartimaeus . . . a blind beggar" was healed? No, one is simply more specific than the other, giving the man's name and identifying him as a beggar. Then, do either of these accounts exclude the possibility that a companion of this man, another blind beggar, was healed at the same time, as Matthew indicated by referring to "two blind men"? Again, there is no conflict; simply additional facts and a different viewpoint.—Matthew 20:29-34; Mark 10:46-52; Luke 18:35-43.

But what about the location where the healing took place? Matthew and Mark say it was when Jesus was "going out" of Jericho. Luke, however, says that it occurred when Jesus was "getting near" Jericho. That is not simply added detail, is it? There seems to be a contradiction. But is there really? Consider this interesting report in the book *Archaeology and Bible History:*

> "Early in the twentieth century A. D., excavations were made at Jericho by Ernest Sellin of the German Oriental Society (1907-1909). The excavations showed that the Jericho of Jesus' time was a double city. The old Jewish city was about a mile away from the Roman city."—1950, p. 295.

So, then, may it not be that Jesus met the beggars while *leaving* the Jewish city and *approaching* the Roman city, or vice versa? A knowledge of the circumstances that existed at the time of writing helps one to appreciate the viewpoint of the writer. It also clears up what might appear to be a contradiction when viewed centuries later without such background knowledge.

CONTEXT OFTEN CLEARS UP SEEMING CONTRADICTIONS

When a question is raised as to the meaning of texts that appear to conflict, it is always wise to examine the context or surrounding material. Perhaps you yourself have had the experience of being misrepresented because something you said was taken out of context. You can appreciate, then, that any use of a scripture in a way that is not in harmony with its context would misrepresent it.

To illustrate, John 1:18 reads: "No man has seen God at any time." Yet Exodus 24:9, 10 says: "Moses and Aaron, Nadab and Abihu and seventy of the older men of Israel proceeded to go up, and they got to see the God of Israel." Do these texts conflict? Removed from context, they may appear to. The next verse in Exodus, however, provides a clarifying detail, saying: "They got a *vision* of the true God." So they did not personally or literally see God, did they?

Reading the context also answers the common

question: Where did Cain, the first son of Adam and Eve, get his wife? (Genesis 4:1, 2, 17) Was not Eve, his mother, the only woman on earth? No; for in giving a recapitulation of Adam's life, Genesis 5:1-5 tells us that Adam "became father to sons and *daughters.*" Obviously, then, Cain took one of his sisters as a wife. Marriage among the offspring of the original human pair was the divine arrangement for populating the earth. (Genesis 1:28; 2:23, 24) And at that time, when man was much closer to the physical perfection with which Adam began life, such marriages would not have adversely affected the offspring as brother-sister marriages often would in our day.

Another example is that of the two genealogies of Jesus' ancestry presented by Matthew and Luke. (Matthew 1:1-16; Luke 3:23-38) Although in some sections of both lists the names coincide, most of them differ. But are they contradictory? Matthew and Luke were both early members of the Christian congregation. So, the one who wrote his account last certainly knew what the other had already recorded. It is obvious, therefore, that these differences were intentional. What, then, could be the reason?

If we read the context we will note that Matthew gives Joseph, Jesus' foster father, considerably more mention than Mary. He tells of Joseph's concern on learning of Mary's pregnancy, how God revealed to him the meaning of this, how he was warned to take his wife and her child to Egypt, and that he later brought the family to Nazareth. Reading Luke's account, however, we see that it deals to a far greater extent with Mary, Joseph being mentioned only incidentally. We read of Mary's receiving a message from God's angel, her visit to her cousin Elizabeth, her song of praise to Jehovah, her giving birth to her son, and her treasuring up the sayings of the visiting shepherds.

So there seems to be good reason to believe that Matthew traced Jesus' genealogy through Joseph as his foster father, while Luke traced the ancestry through Mary's line of descent. Why do this? Again the context aids in understanding. Both accounts establish the fact that Jesus was of the royal line of King David, having a legal right to kingship through his foster father Joseph and a natural right through his actual mother Mary. Thus Jesus' position as David's royal heir was doubly enforced.

Reading the context, then, helps to clear up seeming contradictions, and helps one to get a proper view of the Bible.

THE PROPER VIEW OF APPARENT CONTRADICTIONS

The examples that have been considered here illustrate that a reasonable explanation can generally be found for supposed contradictions. In each case examined it became evident that the Bible itself is not inconsistent. In view of this, what should you do if someday you come across other Bible statements that appear to conflict with each other?

In all fairness to yourself and to the Bible, read first what the Bible itself really says. Many times you will find that any supposed difficulty is based on a misunderstanding. Consider the surrounding verses to determine the subject being discussed and the viewpoint of the writer. Take into account the time the event occurred and the conditions existing then. Look up related portions of the Bible to see what they say. This you can do by using a Bible concordance. But what if even these steps do not lead you to a satisfying explanation?

It is well to keep in mind that, though a problem may appear difficult and even unsolvable to one person, this does not necessarily mean that it cannot be solved. Someone else who has a more thorough knowledge of the Scriptures may quickly and easily find a solution. A person working a problem in algebra, for example, may find no way to solve it by himself. Yet someone else may point out a very simple solution. Surely a beginner in algebra would not say that his textbook was unreliable because he could not at the start solve one of the advanced problems. So, too, with the Scriptures. If you encounter difficult problems, discuss them with someone else, someone who has respect for the Bible and a good knowledge of its contents. Realize, too, that a background of personal knowledge is often necessary in order to appreciate the wisdom manifest in answers that are given. Be patient.

As you continue to read the Bible, you may find that even its seeming contradictions, though comparatively few and minor, take on a new significance for you. Instead of their giving rise to doubts, they may become a reason for faith. How so? *Because such variations are evidence that there was no collusion among the Bible writers.* Obviously, no one has "doctored up" the record. The Bible account, containing the testimony of many witnesses, bears the stamp of truth. It is consistent. This gives added reason for believing that the Bible is what it professes to be—the Word of God.

CHAPTER 8

The Bible's Moral Standards —Are They Consistent?

WHY is it that anyone would question the Bible's moral standards? Do not the Scriptures forbid murder, adultery, stealing and bearing false witness against one's fellowman? Moreover, the Bible even goes far beyond what human laws can enforce. It commands that one should not even desire what belongs to his fellowman and that he should love his neighbor as he does himself. —Exodus 20:13-17; Mark 12:31.

But some persons feel that the moral tone of these requirements is not consistent with other portions of the Bible. They object: "How can I believe that the Bible is from God when it contains, not only a fine moral code, but also reports about such things as Noah getting drunk, Amnon raping his half sister Tamar and other shocking incidents?"

EXAMPLES OF WRONG CONDUCT

Reason on the matter: Why does the Bible report on such events? Is it to provide "entertainment" that appeals to immoral minds or to stimulate others to engage in such conduct?

When, for example, it tells of Noah's becoming drunk, is it encouraging the reader to do the same? In the account at Genesis 9:20-27 you will find nothing that makes the experience sound the least bit desirable. Rather, the things highlighted are the misconduct to which this opened the way for certain of Noah's offspring, with bad repercussions, and also the respectful conduct of others, with resulting blessings. Similarly, in relating the violation of Tamar by Amnon, the Bible makes a point of the deep shame experienced by Tamar and shows that Amnon lost his life because of what he did. (2 Samuel 13:1-29) The account certainly does not move a person to want to engage in the same conduct himself.

Why, then, does the Bible include such accounts of wrongdoing? We can learn valuable lessons from them. These examples, the apostle Paul said, were "written for a warning to us." (1 Corinthians 10:11) They impress on our minds the value of the high moral standards clearly stated in other parts of the Bible.—Proverbs 20:1; 1 Corinthians 6:9, 10.

Moreover, in recording events that expose the sins of those described as God's servants, the Bible displays an honesty and integrity unknown among the Egyptian, Assyrian and other ancient historians. Even today, how many authors expose their own sins? Yet the Bible writers did! Moses frankly told of his own faults and those of his own people. The sins of prominent people, such as David, Solomon, the apostle Peter and others, were not covered over.

This honesty and frankness is entirely consistent with the Bible's being a book of truth and of high moral standards. You would not expect the Word of God to distort or hide the truth, would you? So, when someone criticizes the Bible because it does not suppress the truth, does the fault lie with the Bible or with the one criticizing its honesty? In this regard, columnist Sydney J. Harris, under the heading "Utter Honesty of the Bible," wrote:

> "If the book were merely a smooth piece of religious propaganda, the compilers could easily have removed all the offensive passages . . .
>
> "Street-corner atheists who jubilantly point to such passages as 'proof' that the Bible is a barbarous and inconsistent book are making a defect out of what is really a virtue. . . .
>
> "No other book ever written has vibrated with more agonizing honesty."[34]

WHY THERE MAY SEEM TO BE INCONSISTENCIES

The Bible presents a record of what are said to be God's dealings with mankind during thousands of years. It describes those who pleased him and those who displeased him, those gaining his favor and those meriting his disapproval or condemnation. If, as the evidence thus far indicates, the Bible truly is God's Word, then by studying this record we can come to know God and learn how to please him. Is this what we sincerely want? Not everyone investigating the Bible has this motive.

Some persons approach the Bible with the idea that what it says should conform to their own personal concept. This, of course, will cause difficulty. Why? Because the Bible shows God as saying: "As the heavens are higher than the earth, so my ways are higher than your ways, and my thoughts than your thoughts." (Isaiah 55:9) The Bible further shows all of us to be imperfect, subject to error. (Romans 3:23) Human experience surely demonstrates this. If, then, a person views matters from the standpoint of imperfect human thinking, the Bible's presentation of God's actions in some cases may seem strange, even inconsistent. But if the Bible conformed to our own limited human viewpoint, would that prove it to be from God? How can we be benefited or helped by it if we seek nothing but confirmation of the views we already hold? Reasonably, a book that is God's Word should correct, clarify and elevate our thinking.

The Bible quotes disobedient Israelites as criticizing God's dealings, saying: "The way of Jehovah is not adjusted right." God's reply to them was:

> "As for my ways, are they not adjusted right, O house of Israel? Are not the ways of you people the ones that are not adjusted right? . . . [Turn back] from all your transgressions, and let nothing prove to be for you people a stumbling block causing error."—Ezekiel 18:29, 30.

If we acknowledge that we today are no more in position to act as judges of God than were those Israelites, then we can approach the Bible with the hope of genuine enlightenment. For examples of the valuable lessons that may be learned, consider the Bible account of the execution of the Canaanites—an account that for some has served as a "stumbling block."

GOD'S DECREE AGAINST THE CANAANITES

Review, first, the highlights of that account: After delivering the Israelites from bondage to Egypt, Jehovah led them to the land of Canaan. Some four hundred years earlier God had solemnly promised this land to faithful Abraham and his descendants. Jehovah kept that promise. He now commissioned the Israelites as his executioners of the peoples inhabiting Canaan. (Deuteronomy 7:2; Joshua 10:40) Entire tribes were to be destroyed. Why? Moses explained: "It is for the wickedness of these nations that Jehovah your God is driving them away from before you, and in order to carry out the word that Jehovah swore to your forefathers, Abraham, Isaac and Jacob." (Deuteronomy 9:5) A few Canaanite cities and individuals, however, recognized that Israel had divine backing, came over to their side, and were spared.

What, then, do we learn from this? Does this account in any way indicate that Jehovah is not a God of love and a "lover of justice," as stated elsewhere in the Bible?—1 John 4:8; Psalm 37:28.

No, instead it teaches a vital principle: that God's love of righteousness has as its counterpart a hatred of wickedness. Read Leviticus chapter 18 and consider the "detestable" practices of the Canaanites for which God would cause the land to 'vomit them out.' There are also additional historical sources to show us what kind of people they were. Professor Merrill F. Unger observes:

> "The brutality, lust and abandon of Canaanite mythology is far worse than elsewhere in the Near East at the time. And the astounding characteristic of Canaanite deities, that they had no moral character whatever, must have brought out the worst traits in their devotees and entailed many of the most demoralizing practices of the time, such as sacred prostitution, child sacrifice and snake worship.
>
> " . . . The character of Canaanite religion as portrayed in the Ugaritic literature furnishes ample background to illustrate the accuracy of . . . Biblical statements in their characterization of the utter moral and religious degeneracy of the inhabitants of Canaan."[35]

Surely it is not reasonable to think that God's love for mankind would oblige him to be a lover of wickedness too.

Yet, God's opposition to wickedness is not the only principle stressed. The account also shows that God is not quick to destroy imperfect people at the first evidence of transgression. God had noted the iniquity of the Amorite inhabitants of Canaan some four hundred years before, but did not then destroy them. (Genesis 15:13-21) This accords with other Bible evidence that God 'takes no pleasure in the death of the wicked,' but mercifully affords opportunity for people to change their wrong ways. (Ezekiel 33:11; Psalm 103:8) Rather than repel us, then, this account can reassure us, draw us to God. At the same time, his execution of the Canaanites should satisfy us that God does not shut his eyes to wrongdoing. This gives sound basis for believing that he will not forever tolerate the wickedness that is now making the earth an increasingly corrupt and dangerous place to live.

Someone may say, however: "But not only men and women were destroyed among the Canaanites. Even little children were put to death." This is true. Is this inconsistent on God's part? Is there anything worth while to be learned in this? And, most vital for us, are we willing to face up to the facts revealed and 'adjust our ways' to sound and righteous principles? Let us see.

The Bible shows that God places full responsibility on parents for the minor children they have procreated. Such responsibility is a divine privilege. It is also a divine obligation, one that parents can neither avoid nor transfer with God's approval. God held to this same principle with the Israelites, saying:

> "I have put life and death before you, the blessing and the malediction; and you must choose life in order that you may keep alive, you *and your offspring,* by loving Jehovah your God, by listening to his voice and by sticking to him."—Deuteronomy 30:19, 20.

By their obedience or disobedience the Israelites could choose either life or death for themselves and their children.

It is an undeniable fact of life that children benefit or suffer according to what their parents are and do. If a parent is upright, conscientious, and lovingly concerned with the welfare of his family, both materially and spiritually, the children benefit greatly. If he is not, the children inevitably suffer. Some may wish this were otherwise. The immoral man risks the possibility of contracting a venereal disease. If this happens, can he rightly expect God to screen off his children, born or unborn, from the damaging effects of the disease he contracts? If a man is lazy or a drunkard, can he rightly expect God to take over his obligation or assign it to others so that no suffering comes to his offspring? And would it be *consistent* for God to cooperate with such men in an evasion of their responsibility? Upon whom, then, should the blame for the children's suffering rest? The Bible shows that this responsibility rests precisely where God put it—on the parents.

What, then, of the Canaanite parents? They, too, could choose either life or death, blessing or cursing, for themselves and their children. The Canaanite inhabitants of four cities submitted to God's will, as did Rahab of Jericho and her family. They recognized the hand of the true God in the events taking place, and they took their stand in association with God's people. For this they and their children survived. (Joshua 2:1-21; 6:25; 9:3-27) The other Canaanite parents could have done the same but they refused. (Numbers 21:21-24) By so doing they chose death for themselves and for their children.

Thus a vital lesson is presented for us now. While some parents today may contend that Jehovah's ways 'are not adjusted right,' it may well be asked if the ways of today's parents are adjusted right. Why does juvenile delinquency increase earth wide, characterized by disrespect, immorality and crimes, some extremely vicious? Many law authorities place the primary responsibility where the Bible places it—on negligent parents. On the other hand, according to the Bible, any parent who is willing to do so, whose love for God, for himself and for his family is sufficiently strong, can learn to live by godly principles. He can bring up his minor children "in the discipline and authoritative advice of Jehovah." (Ephesians 6:4) The Bible states that, when God cleans out wickedness from the whole earth, such parents will have chosen life for themselves and for their children.—1 Corinthians 7:14; 2 Thessalonians 1:6-10.

IS THE CHRISTIAN STANDARD DIFFERENT?

What about the view of some that the requirements set out in the Hebrew Scriptures are inconsistent with those given to Christians?

The Bible shows that God has not given the same instructions to his servants at every period of human history. Noah was instructed to build an ark, but the global flood of his day is not to be repeated. (Genesis 9:11) So, too, God gave the nation of Israel a body of laws, but that Law covenant was binding only on them. (Psalm 147:19, 20; Exodus 31:16, 17) Thus, the Bible states that Christians are not under the Mosaic law because, as Romans 10:4 explains, "Christ is the end of the Law." Why is that?

It is not because God's principles have changed. Galatians 3:24 points out: "Consequently the Law has become our tutor leading to Christ, that we might be declared righteous due to faith." The things set out in the Law were said to be "a shadow of the things to come, but the reality belongs to the Christ." (Colossians 2:17) So, while the requirements for the Jews under the Law and those outlined for Christians differ, they do not conflict. The Jewish arrangement contained a prophetic pattern that is fulfilled in the Christian system.—Hebrews 10:1.

"But is not even the *moral standard* different?" someone may ask. "Did not the Mosaic law encourage retaliation, 'soul for soul, and eye for eye'? (Deuteronomy 19:21) How different from Christian forgiveness!" But is it?

First, note that this law was not urging an Israelite to seek personal vengeance, taking the law into his own hands. To the contrary, God's willingness to accept sacrifices and forgive the Israelites set the pattern for them to forgive one another. (Leviticus 4:20) But "eye for eye" pertained to judgments to be rendered, not by some individual, but by the appointed legal judges of the nation in cases of wrongdoing. (Exodus 21: 1, 22-25) The just enforcement of this law would certainly prove to be a strong deterrent to malicious attacks that might cripple innocent persons. It would encourage a deep respect for the person of one's fellowman. In our day, when criminal attacks are a growing menace, can we not appreciate the wisdom of such a deterrent? However, there is yet another aspect to the matter. What is that?

The Bible shows that Jehovah God, the Supreme Judge, himself adhered to this principle of 'soul for soul.' He did this in providing relief from the damaging effects of the first man Adam's rebellion. By his own sin, Adam brought sin and its penalty death upon all his offspring. Only if someone not himself a sinner would give his life or "soul" to cancel out that penalty could divine justice be satisfied and mankind be redeemed from death. God did not inconsistently nullify his sentence pronounced against Adam in Eden. But, in harmony with the legal principle of 'soul for soul,' he provided a means of salvation for Adam's offspring through the ransom sacrifice of his own Son Jesus Christ. (Romans 5:12; 1 Timothy 2:5; John 3:16) Thus, this principle lies at the very heart of Christianity.

As for personal vengeance, the exhortation is given to Christians: "Do not avenge yourselves, beloved, but yield place to the wrath." Note, too, that this scripture backs up this exhortation by quoting the Mosaic law, saying: "For it is written [at Deuteronomy 32:35, 41]: 'Vengeance is mine; I will repay, says Jehovah.'" (Romans 12:19) So, then, both in the Jewish nation and among Christians encouragement was given to trust in God's own arrangement for the correction and punishment of wrongdoing.

What of the charge made by some that "the Old Testament presents God as a God of war but the New Testament presents him as a God of peace"? Investigation shows this charge to be misleading in both points.

The Hebrew Scriptures do contain accounts of warfare. But they also are the source of major prophecies concerning the "Prince of Peace" and his government of peace which the "zeal of Jehovah of armies" would establish.—Isaiah 9:6, 7; Psalm 72:1-7; Micah 4:1-4.

True, God did not commission Christians to act as his executioners, as he did the Israelites. The Bible shows that he assigned them a spiritual warfare, fought with the "sword of the spirit," the Word of God. (Ephesians 6:10-17) Also, Christians would have no earthly kingdom, as the Jews had, but would be a spiritual nation with members in all parts of the earth. So, they were to live as peaceful, law-abiding subjects under the many existing governments. (Romans 13:1-7; 1 Peter 2:9-17) But God would still war against the wicked, executing judgment on them in his war of Armageddon, although using, not humans, but angels as executioners. God's own Son, Christ Jesus, would take the lead in 'shepherding the nations with a rod of iron.' (2 Thessalonians 1:6-10; Revelation 16:13-16; 19:11-16) The Christian Greek Scriptures make clear that only by this means would 'God's will be done on earth as it is in heaven,' to the blessing of those who love righteousness. (Matthew 6:10) God's purpose concerning war and peace is therefore consistent in both the Hebrew and the Christian Greek Scriptures.

MAKING MANIFEST WHAT IS IN ONE'S HEART

The way in which the Bible is written and the things it contains probe deeply into human hearts and produce revealing reactions. The Bible itself says: "The word of God is alive and exerts power and is sharper than any two-edged sword . . . and is able to discern thoughts and intentions of the heart. . . . all things are naked and openly exposed to the eyes of him with whom we have an accounting." (Hebrews 4:12, 13) If we incline to view our own personal desires and concepts as more important than the Creator's purposes and standards for all mankind, perhaps being guided by sentiment rather than right principles—is it not reasonable that the Word of God would reveal this?

In some cases the Bible gives detailed reasons why God took certain actions that affected, favorably or adversely, the lives of men. In others, it does not. Some persons may reject the entire Bible because one passage does not contain sufficient details to satisfy them. But is such distrust warranted?

When we examine the Bible's moral standards, not superficially, but carefully, do we not find reflected in them a wisdom higher than human wisdom? They explain why the Almighty Creator of this vast universe has patiently waited this long to put an end to wrongdoing on this small planet Earth. (Exodus 9:16; 2 Peter 3:8, 9; Revelation 11:18) The Bible spells out in detail the loving purpose of God toward mankind; it reveals the progressive steps he has taken to bring lasting relief for those who want to live according to what is right and true. (Galatians 4:4; 1 John 4:9, 10; Revelation 21:4, 5) In plain language that even a child can understand, the Bible sets out God's basic requirements for those who would please him, requirements within the reach of all. (John 17:3; Micah 6:8) It consistently encourages its readers to meet those requirements, to choose life, not death, for themselves and their families.—Joshua 24:15.

So, then, why do some persons view portions of the Bible as a stumbling block, a hindrance to their accepting it? Is it because the revelation of God contained therein is really inconsistent or lacks stability? No, the facts are to the contrary. Then could their objections be because of the changes in their own lives that acceptance of the Bible as God's Word would require? Few would openly say this. But the Bible shows that the heart is where the problem usually lies. —Proverbs 4:23; Jeremiah 17:9, 10; Mark 3:1-6.

We rightly expect the Word of God to be consistent. We also expect it to be firm and not apologetic, yet warm and understanding. With an open mind and an open heart, read the Bible and examine the way it meets those standards.

CHAPTER 9

The Significance of Bible Prophecy

PROPHECY is one of the outstanding features of the Bible. In its pages God is revealed as the "One telling from the beginning the finale, and from long ago the things that have not been done." (Isaiah 46:10) Centuries in advance the Bible foretold which kingdoms would dominate the international scene, and the order in which they would appear. It named men before they were born and told in detail acts they would perform. It set out advance notice of acts of God. More strikingly perhaps than any other feature, prophecy distinguishes the Bible from all other ancient sacred writings. This has, as we shall see, great significance.

"But," you may ask, "were there not other prophets in ancient times aside from the Hebrew prophets of the Bible?" Yes, there were. However, as Professor G. R. Berry of Colgate University comments:

> "No important written records of the utterances of any of these prophets outside of the Hebrew people have been preserved. . . . Prophecy among other nations aside from the Hebrews was ordinarily of the clairvoyant type, being given in answer to specific questions of individuals, and hence of no general or permanent value."[36]

History shows that the soothsayers and oracles of the ancient Greeks and other ancient peoples were more like the fortune-tellers of modern times. They did not go to the people with prophetic messages from God. They waited for individuals to come to them, seeking answers to personal questions about their future. The answers, couched in vague terms, came only after the seeker had financed costly ceremonies and offerings. Those without money went away without any prediction. Bible prophecy, by contrast, was and is free for all persons.—Isaiah 55:1-3; Revelation 22:17.

INSPIRED PROPHECY OR HUMAN PREDICTIONS—WHICH?

Some persons express doubts. They say: "Are the prophecies of the Bible really inspired of God? Or are they perhaps simply clever predictions made by men on the basis of what they saw as to observable trends? Isn't it true that even today men can predict what course a certain nation is going to take?"

Men can make predictions, and they are sometimes right. Like players in a chess game, they can at times use shrewd analysis to forecast the future moves of a government. But they are often wrong. It is quite another thing to foretell with precision a series of major events that go completely contrary to what all signs apparently indicate. And it is beyond the power of man to do this *centuries in advance*. Has the Bible really done this? And has it done this, not as a hit-and-miss affair, but with unfailing accuracy? If it has, then there can be no honest denial that the Bible is the inspired Word of God. We invite you to consider the evidence.

LONG-RANGE PROPHECIES CONCERNING BABYLON AND JERUSALEM

Back in the eighth century B.C.E. the prophet Isaiah wrote that he had been instructed by God to foretell things concerning Babylon. In prophecy he depicted Babylon as head of a powerful empire, the "Mistress of Kingdoms." And Isaiah also foretold that this empire would overrun the land of Judah and its capital Jerusalem, laying it waste and carrying its people into exile.—Isaiah 24:1-3; 39:3-7; 47:5.

Yet in Isaiah's day Babylon was only a second-rate power, a mere satellite of the mighty Assyrian Empire. Not until a full century later did Babylon gain the ascendancy over Assyria and become the dominant power in the Middle East. Scores of years after Isaiah had passed off the scene, Babylonian King Nebuchadnezzar besieged Jerusalem. He battered it to the ground, thoroughly wasting and depopulating the land of Judah.

The prophet Jeremiah, about eighteen years before Jerusalem's destruction, had given this warning of the coming exile:

> "And all this land must become a devastated place, an object of astonishment, and these nations will have to serve the king of Babylon seventy years."—Jeremiah 25:1, 2, 8-11; compare 2 Chronicles 36:20, 21.

In the early part of this twentieth century, some critics did not believe that it happened that way. But after a half century of archaeological research, what is the view now? Archaeologist W. F. Albright says:

> "Excavation and surface exploration in Judah have proved that the towns of Judah were not only completely destroyed by the Chaldeans in their two

invasions, but were not reoccupied for generations —often never again in history."[37]

The prophecy was unerringly fulfilled. Can this be explained away as simply shrewd reasoning or analysis on Jeremiah's part?

But this is not all. Isaiah announced the divine decree that Babylon would fall to the Medes, with whom the Persians were associated. He even recorded the very name of the future leader of the conquering army: Cyrus—and that some two hundred years in advance, long before Cyrus was even born!—Isaiah chapters 13 and 14; also 44:26-28.

Babylon was built astraddle the river Euphrates. A vast system of canals and moats surrounded it. Immense gates and walls protected it. So how could Cyrus take this virtually impregnable city? The Bible prophecies said:

"This is what Jehovah has said to his anointed one, to Cyrus, whose right hand I have taken hold of, to subdue before him nations, . . . to open before him the two-leaved doors, so that even the gates will not be shut."—Isaiah 45:1.

"There is a sword . . . against the inhabitants of Babylon . . . a devastation upon her waters, and they must be dried up." "The mighty men of Babylon have ceased to fight. . . . One runner runs to meet another runner, and one reporter to meet another reporter, to report to the king of Babylon that his city has been captured at every end, and that the fords themselves have been seized."—Jeremiah 50:35-38; 51:30-32.

What *did* happen? Did these prophecies come true? Note what the Greek historian Herodotus wrote after the events took place:

"Cyrus . . . diverted the river by means of a canal, into the lake, which was before a swamp, he made the ancient channel fordable by the sinking of the river. When this took place, the Persians

... entered Babylon by this passage. If, however, the Babylonians had been aware of it beforehand, or had known what Cyrus was about, they would not have suffered the Persians to enter the city, but would have utterly destroyed them; for, having shut all the little gates that lead down to the river, and mounting the walls that extend along the banks of the river, they would have caught them as in a net; whereas the Persians came upon them by surprise. It is related by the people who inhabited this city, that, by reason of its great extent, when they who were at the extremities were taken, those of the Babylonians who inhabited the centre knew nothing of the capture (for it happened to be a festival); but they were dancing at the time, and enjoying themselves, till they received certain information of the truth. And thus Babylon was taken."—*Herodotus,* Book I, sec. 191; compare Daniel 5:1-4, 30.

Xenophon, another ancient historian, gives a similar account. He tells of Cyrus' diverting the waters of the Euphrates, sending his forces up the riverbed past the city walls, catching the guards unawares and taking the city in one night. —*Cyropaedia,* VII, 5:7-34.

The Bible prophecies were fulfilled to the letter! Babylon's fall came in 539 B.C.E., some *fifty years* after the time of Jeremiah's prophecy and nearly *two hundred years* after Isaiah's day! How, then, could these prophecies possibly be the result of mere human wisdom?

THE PROPHET DANIEL AND ALEXANDER THE GREAT

While the Jews were in exile in Babylon, the prophet Daniel received startling visions concerning the future. These visions forecast the march of mighty world powers for centuries to come. Daniel foresaw the fall of the Medo-Persian Empire, symbolized in the vision by a two-horned ram (a dual power). How would it fall? Daniel foretold that its defeat would result from a swift onslaught by Greece, represented by a male goat with a great horn. (Daniel 8:1-7, 20, 21) Note now what was foretold to follow:

"And the male of the goats, for its part, put on great airs to an extreme; but as soon as it became mighty, the great horn was broken, and there proceeded to come up conspicuously four instead of it, toward the four winds of the heavens." —Daniel 8:8.

What did this mean? The explanation given in Daniel's prophetic writing is:

"The hairy he-goat stands for the king of Greece; and as for the great horn that was between its eyes, it stands for the first king. And that one having been broken, so that there were four that finally stood up instead of it, there are four kingdoms from his nation that will stand up, but not with his power."

"His kingdom will be broken and be divided toward the four winds of the heavens, but not to his posterity and not according to his dominion with which he had ruled."—Daniel 8:21, 22; 11:3, 4.

Have you read the history of the Grecian Empire? If you have, then you know that the following is what took place:

After some two centuries of domination, the Medo-Persian Empire was overthrown by the lightning campaign of Alexander the Great, at the head of the Greek forces. He demolished the Medo-Persian power in 331 B.C.E. Intending to make conquered Babylon his capital, Alexander fell victim to malaria and died in 323 B.C.E. at the age of thirty-two. As foretold, he died 'as soon as he became mighty' as world ruler!

Alexander had an infant son by a princess named Roxana, as well as an illegitimate son by a certain Barsine. But the vision given Daniel foretold that the kingdom would go "not to his posterity and not according to his dominion with which he had ruled." To whom did it go?

Though Alexander's brother and sons tried to control the kingdom, they could not succeed. Within a few years after Alexander's death and after the decisive battle of Ipsus, his empire was split up among four of his generals. They were Seleucus Nicator, Cassander, Ptolemy Lagus, and Lysimachus. Yet, as foretold, none of these ever had the power that the "first king" Alexander possessed.

Is this 'mere historical coincidence'? A reasoning mind cannot accept such an assertion. Nor can the accuracy of such long-range prophecy be paralleled by anything that sources outside the Bible can offer. The prophecies of Daniel turned the Biblical spotlight on those world events two hundred years before they occurred.* Note, too, that Daniel gave the credit to God, even admitting that he did not fully understand certain prophecies given him: "Now as for me, I heard, but I could not understand."—Daniel 12:8.

HISTORY DISGUISED AS PROPHECY?

Confronted with this evidence of divine inspiration, some modern critics have dismissed the prophecies, referring to them as 'merely history parading as prophecy.' They claim that these writings were recorded after the events took place and not before. What can be said of such charges?

First, upon investigation it becomes evident that the critics cannot prove their claims. They

* For details of Daniel's prophecies about the rise and fall of world empires see the book *"Your Will Be Done on Earth,"* chapters 5 and 8.

say that large sections of the writings of the prophets—Isaiah, Jeremiah, Ezekiel, Daniel and others—are fraudulent, being the work of "later hands." But they have neither witnesses nor sound evidence to support their charge. If there were such "later hands," who were they? They cannot identify them; history knows nothing of them.

Nor can the critics bring forth any reasonable motive for making false additions to these Bible books. Care of the Holy Scriptures was entrusted to the Aaronic priesthood of Israel. If false additions were made, it would have had to be with their cooperation. But why should they cooperate in such a fraud? If anything, they might prefer to keep such prophecies out of the Sacred Writings. Why? Because these very prophecies contain some of the strongest denunciations ever made of the Jewish priesthood for their frequent unfaithfulness.

For example, God there describes Israel's priests as 'blind watchmen,' shepherds with no understanding, interested only in "unjust gain," "acting falsely," and profaning "what was holy." (Isaiah 56:10, 11; Jeremiah 8:10; Zephaniah 3:4) Surely if deceitful priests had "doctored up" any of these books they would at the same time have eliminated such unfavorable references to the religious leaders. On the other hand, if those making the claimed "adjustments" in these books were sincere, devoted priests, is it reasonable to believe that they would stoop to fraud in handling God's Word?

Furthermore, if such prophecies were actually fraudulent additions, why were they never doubted by the Jewish people? In those ancient times writings were comparatively rare, and making copies was costly. So anything new would arouse a far greater degree of attention than at the present. And any fraudulent additions would have stirred up a controversy that would have been a matter of historical record.

Among the Jews, reverence for authentic Sacred Writings was outstanding. A number of apocryphal works, including the histories of the Maccabean Wars, were excluded by them from the sacred canon of inspired books. This very fact shows that they were on guard against anything that did not give clear evidence of divine inspiration.

Significantly, not even the modern critics would attempt to say that any of the Bible prophecies in the Hebrew Scriptures were written later than the second century B.C.E. Why not? For one thing, what are known as the Dead Sea Scrolls have been discovered, and these ancient documents are accepted as dating back to the first or second century before our Common Era. Among other Bible books, they contain the prophecy of Isaiah. An even stronger reason, however, is that the first translation of the Hebrew Scriptures into the Greek language had already got under way before the second century B.C.E. This translation, called the "Septuagint Version," contained all the prophetic books that we have today. These facts deal a crushing blow to the claim that the prophecies were rewritten to conform with history. How so?

This is because the historical events fulfilling certain prophecies came long after the *Septuagint Version* was completed. Consider some examples of these prophecies.

A CITY NEVER TO BE REINHABITED

What would you think if someone were to foretell that a major city of the world, such as London, Rome, New York or Moscow, would become a mere wasteland and *never* be rebuilt? Yet that is what was foretold concerning Babylon, the onetime capital of the world. Bible prophecy decreed that it would become "piles of stones" and a place for jackals and owls to dwell. It would "never be inhabited" again!—Jeremiah 51:37; Isaiah 13:20-22; 14:22, 23.

Was this just 'history parading as prophecy'? Impossible. Why? Because Babylon was still inhabited as far down as the first century C.E. Furthermore, it was most unlikely that a city such as Babylon would become forever uninhabited. As archaeologists well know, when ancient cities were destroyed, new ones were usually built on the same sites, particularly if favorably situated. And Babylon's favorable situation made it one of the greatest cities of all history. Despite this, the prophecy came true.

For, finally, in the early part of the Common Era, the entire city of Babylon did indeed become "piles of stones." André Parrot, head curator of the French National Museums, described the present-day site in this way:

> "The town is only a short distance from Baghdad, and a stream of tourists pours into it almost daily. They are generally deeply disappointed and almost with one voice exclaim that there is nothing to see. They expect to find palaces, temples, and the 'Tower of Babel'; they are shown only masses of ruins, . . . grey-coloured and crumbling, and in no way impressive. The destruction wrought by man has been completed by the ravages of nature . . . No human power can arrest this ceaseless spolia-

tion. It is no longer possible to reconstruct Babylon; her destiny is accomplished."[38]

Uninhabited—a place for tourists to stop, view the ruins, and then be picked up later and travel on. Could Isaiah or Jeremiah have enforced the divine decree contained in the prophecies they wrote? Obviously not. But the Inspirer of those prophecies, Jehovah God, could enforce their fulfillment and has done so.

NATIONS THAT DISAPPEARED

Many ancient races and nations have continued in existence for thousands of years as identifiable peoples. You perhaps have met Jews, Greeks, Egyptians or Ethiopians. But have you ever met anyone of the Moabite, Ammonite or Edomite races? No? Neither has anyone else in modern times. Why not? Because Bible prophecy foretold that "Edom must become an object of astonishment. . . . Just as in the overthrow of Sodom and Gomorrah." (Jeremiah 49:17, 18) And God's prophet also said: "Moab herself will become just like Sodom, and the sons of Ammon like Gomorrah, a place possessed by nettles, and a salt pit, and a desolate waste, even to time indefinite."—Zephaniah 2:9.

Again, you can investigate for yourself. You will find that, though remnants of these peoples continued down into the Common Era, their nations never revived. They eventually disappeared, assimilated by Arab tribes. Their end came centuries *after*, not before, the completion of the Hebrew Scriptures.

THE MESSIANIC PROPHECIES

For thousands of years, descendants of Abraham looked for the coming of the promised "Seed of Abraham," the Messiah. Over the centuries, prophecies concerning this Coming One built up a picture of what he would be like and what he would do. (Acts 3:20-24) It was centuries after the last book of the Hebrew Scriptures was written that this whole body of prophecies began to undergo fulfillment. They saw their realization in Jesus Christ.

In the book *Archaeology and Bible History,* Professor J. P. Free presents an estimate of the number of distinct prophecies of the Hebrew Scriptures that were fulfilled in Jesus Christ. How many? 332! Commenting on this, he states:

> "The chances of all these prophecies being fulfilled in one man are so overwhelmingly remote that it is strikingly demonstrated that they could in no wise be the shrewd guesses of mere men." —1950, p. 284.

Following is a chart of just a few of these Bible prophecies, giving their location in the Hebrew Scriptures and the texts in the Christian Greek Scriptures showing their fulfillment in Jesus:

Hebrew Scriptures	Prophecy	Fulfillment
Genesis 49:10; Isaiah 9:7; 11:1, 10	Born of the tribe of Judah, from the family of David, the son of Jesse	Matthew 1:1-16; Luke 3:23-33
Micah 5:2	Born in Bethlehem	Matthew 2:1, 5, 6
Isaiah 7:14	Born of a virgin	Matthew 1:18-23; Luke 1:30-35
Hosea 11:1	Called out of Egypt	Matthew 2:15
Psalm 78:2	Spoke with parables	Matthew 13:11-13, 31-35
Isaiah 53:1-3; Psalm 69:4	Not believed in; hated without cause	John 12:37, 38; 15:24, 25; Luke 23:13-25

Zechariah 9:9; Psalm 118:26	Entry into Jerusalem on colt of an ass; hailed as king and as coming in Jehovah's name	Matthew 21:1-9; Mark 11:7-11
Psalm 41:9; 109:8; Zechariah 11:12	A trusted companion unfaithful; betrays him for thirty pieces of silver	Matthew 26:15, 47-50; 27:3-10; Acts 1:16-20
Zechariah 13:7	Disciples scatter, abandoning him	Matthew 26:31, 56
Psalm 27:12; Isaiah 53:7	False witnesses used; he remains silent before accusers	Matthew 26:59-61; 27:12-14; Mark 14:56-61; 15:4, 5
Isaiah 50:6; Micah 5:1; Psalm 22:16	Struck, spat on, hands and feet nailed	Matthew 26:67; 27:26, 30; John 20:25
Isaiah 53:12; Psalm 22:18	Numbered with sinners; lots cast for garments	Matthew 26:55, 56; 27:35, 38
Psalm 22:7, 8; 69:21	Reviled while on stake; given vinegar and gall	Matthew 27:34, 39-43, 48; Mark 15:23, 29-32
Isaiah 53:5; Zechariah 12:10; Psalm 34:20	Pierced, but no bones broken	John 19:33-37
Isaiah 53:5, 8, 11, 12	Dies sacrificial death to carry away sins and open way to righteous standing with God	Matthew 20:28; 2 Corinthians 5:21; Hebrews 9:12-15; 1 Peter 2:24
Isaiah 53:9	Buried with the rich	Matthew 27:57-60
Jonah 1:17; Psalm 16:8-11	In grave parts of three days, then resurrected before corruption	Matthew 12:39, 40; 1 Corinthians 15:3, 4

Even this limited number of prophecies could not have been fulfilled by mere chance. However, what of the extreme view of some that Jesus deliberately arranged matters so that the events in his life would fit all these prophecies?

What do you think? Could Jesus have arranged to be born of the tribe of Judah? of a descendant of David? and in the town of David's birth, Bethlehem? No, the very start of his life, which fulfilled these prophecies, was beyond his control.

Could Jesus have arranged for the priests to pay Judas the thirty pieces of silver to betray him? Could he have arranged that his enemies spit in his face, that the Roman authorities sentence him to be nailed to a stake, that the soldiers cast lots for his garments, or that, while piercing his side with a spear, they not follow the custom of breaking certain of his bones?

How, too, could anyone harmonize a fraudulent arranging of matters with the message of Jesus? His Sermon on the Mount and all his other teachings are of a morality of the highest order, unequaled in any other literature, ancient or modern. Who, then, appears to be the shrewd schemer—the accused? or his accusers? And to what works or teachings of *theirs* could the accusers point as evidence that they are not capable of such misrepresentation?

THE GREATEST PROPHET OF THEM ALL

The line of Biblical prophets reached its high point in Jesus Christ. In a remarkable prediction he foretold the total ruin that would come upon Jerusalem because of her unfaithfulness to God and her rejection of Jesus Christ as Messiah.

> "If you, even you, had discerned in this day the things having to do with peace—but now they have been hid from your eyes. Because the days will come upon you when your enemies will build around you a fortification with pointed stakes and will encircle you and distress you from every side, and they will dash you and your children within you to the ground, and they will not leave a stone upon a stone in you, because you did not discern the time of your being inspected."—Luke 19:41-44.

Later, talking to his disciples, he specifically included the temple in the coming desolation. And he warned that, upon seeing the sign of encamped armies around the city, it would be time for them to flee from the doomed city. Here is Jesus' warning prophecy:

"When you see Jerusalem surrounded by encamped armies, then know that the desolating of

Long in advance, Jesus Christ foretold details about Jerusalem's destruction in 70 C.E. He prophesied that, even after the siege began, there would be opportunity to flee. There was, and those who believed the prophecy escaped with their lives.

her has drawn near. Then let those in Judea begin fleeing to the mountains, . . . they will fall by the edge of the sword and be led captive into all the nations; and Jerusalem will be trampled on by the nations."—Luke 21:20-24; Mark 13:2, 14.

However, suppose someone here suggests that the Bible reporters, Mark and Luke, drew up these prophecies after Jerusalem's fall? You are invited to investigate any modern reference works available. You will see that virtually all scholars assign Mark's Gospel account to the decade before 70 C.E., that is, before the date of Jerusalem's fall.

As to Luke, a comparison of Luke 1:1-4 and Acts 1:1 shows that Luke's Gospel was written before the book of Acts. The book of Acts ends with Paul's two-year imprisonment in Rome. (Acts 28:16-31) When was this? The dates for Acts are figured on the basis of the dates credited to Roman authorities involved in the narrative. The earliest date suggested for Paul's imprisonment is about 56-58 C.E., while the latest is about 62-64 C.E. (See *Encyclopædia Britannica,* 1959 edition, Vol. 3, p. 528.) Either of these dates would logically place the time of Luke's writing his Gospel account many years before Jerusalem's fall.

What, then, did happen to Jerusalem? The city revolted against Rome, and the Imperial army marched against it in 66 C.E. The capture of the city seemed certain. But Jesus' words, quoted by Mark and Luke, and also Matthew, indicated there would be opportunity to flee. (Matthew 24:15, 16; Mark 13:14; Luke 21:21) Was there? Yes, for as Josephus, the non-Christian Jewish historian of that time, writes:

"Cestius [the Roman commander] . . . suddenly called off his men, abandoned hope though he had suffered no reverse, and flying in the face of all reason retired from the City."[39]

This humanly unpredictable withdrawal gave Christians the opportunity to obey Jesus' prophetic exhortation and flee the city.

Then what? Around Passover time of the year 70 C.E. General Titus encircled the crowded city with troops and the final siege began. Historian Josephus reports that, at a council of war, Titus urged the building of a wall around the city. His plan was adopted. The countryside around Jerusalem within a radius of about ten miles was denuded of trees and an encircling fence of stakes nearly five miles long was erected in just three days. After some five months of siege, Jerusalem fell.

What would happen to the city and its temple? According to Josephus, an eyewitness of the events, it was contrary to the desires of Titus to destroy the city or its temple. He is quoted as saying to the surviving Jews:

"Most unwillingly I brought engines to bear on your walls: my soldiers, ever thirsting for your blood, I held in leash: after every victory, as if it was a defeat, I appealed to you for an armistice. When I got near to the Temple I again deliberately forwent my rights as victor and appealed to you to spare your own holy places and preserve the Sanctuary for your own use, offering you freedom to come out and a guarantee of safety or, if you wished, a chance to fight on other ground."[40]

But, contrary to the original intentions of the Roman general, the city and its temple were razed to the ground. Only three towers and a portion of the western wall of the city were left standing. Josephus reports:

"All the rest of the fortifications encircling the City were so completely levelled with the ground that no one visiting the spot would believe it had once been inhabited."[41]

What, now, is the significance of all these fulfilled Bible prophecies? For the answer, consider Jesus' words: "I am telling you before it occurs, in order that when it does occur you may believe that I am he." (John 13:19) He claimed to be God's Son, the Messiah, and to verify his claim he not only performed marvelous works but uttered a prophecy about Jerusalem so precise that it could never be fulfilled by mere coincidence. Any one of these fulfilled prophecies is enough to indicate something beyond human ability. The collective force of all the prophecies, taken together, provides overwhelming evidence that only God could inspire them. That, in turn, means that the Bible, which contains these prophecies, must really be the Word of God!

But there is more. Bible prophecies do not deal simply with the ancient past. They are having remarkable fulfillment right now, as we shall see.

CHAPTER 10

Bible Prophecies You Have Seen Fulfilled

YOU did not personally witness the flood of Noah's day. You were not on hand to hear Jesus preach or to see the miracles he performed. Though there is powerful evidence that these events took place, you were not there. However, you have been an eyewitness of one of the most convincing evidences that the Bible is the Word of God. You have personally seen the fulfillment of Bible prophecies in our day.

These prophecies were first spoken by Jesus Christ and his apostles. Some of the major ones are recorded in the Bible at Matthew chapters 24 and 25, Mark 13, Luke 21, 2 Timothy 3 and Revelation 6. They foretold events that would identify the time known as the "last days."

The question may be asked: "But do not some of these prophecies relate to the destruction of Jerusalem by the Romans in 70 C.E.?" Yes, some of those prophecies do. But, in reading them, it becomes evident that they also have an application far beyond that time, to the time of the establishment of God's kingdom under the rule of his Son Christ Jesus. (Luke 21:31-36) That did not take place at the time of Jerusalem's destruction, nor during the years following. How do we know?

For one thing, the book of Revelation makes this clear. The apostle John recorded it near the end of the first century C.E., decades after Jerusalem's fall. Its first verse states that it is "a revelation by Jesus Christ, which God gave him" concerning things that were yet future. (Revelation 1:1) In the Revelation, prophecies described in symbol the future time when Christ Jesus would begin his rule, as well as the start and completion of his conquest of all opposers. (Revelation 6:1, 2; 12:7-12; 19:11–20:3) These prophecies clearly find their fulfillment in our day, as we shall see.

Why does the Bible contain these prophecies? To add to the solid basis for faith. To tell us the meaning of the present violent world conditions. To inform us where we stand in relation to the outworking of God's purposes, and to give us a purpose in life. Seeing the fulfillment of these prophecies, we are helped to recognize the urgency of acting now if we hope to survive the end of this wicked system of things and enter into God's promised new order 'in which righteousness is to dwell.'—2 Peter 3:13.

For the encouragement of lovers of righteousness who would see the fulfillment of these prophecies Jesus said:

> "As these things start to occur, raise yourselves erect and lift your heads up, because your deliverance is getting near."—Luke 21:28.

But what are the events that Jesus foretold?

A "GREAT SWORD" OF WARFARE

As part of a great "sign" of the beginning of his Kingdom rule, Jesus foretold war. There obviously would have to be something notable about the warfare in order for it to form part of a distinctive sign. At Revelation 6:3, 4, it is made plain that such is the case. There the foretold warfare is depicted as a symbolic rider on a red horse, carrying a great sword and 'taking peace away,' not from just a few nations, but "from the earth," so that they should slaughter one another. This runs parallel with Jesus' earlier reference to the rising of 'nation against nation and kingdom against kingdom.'—Matthew 24:6, 7.

Have you seen the prophecy of warfare fulfilled? Yes, for you live in the time when human warfare has changed strikingly. You may even have seen the beginning of this, for it started over a half century ago with what historians called the "Great War" or World War I in 1914-1918. It was the first example of *total* war—warfare on a global scale. World War I differed from all previous wars. As military analyst H. W. Baldwin, in the book *World War I,* points out:

> "In its scope, its violence, and above all, in its totality, it established a precedent. World War I ushered in the century of Total War, of—in the first full sense of the term—global war. . . .
>
> "Never before 1914-1918 had a war absorbed so much of the total resources of so many combatants and covered so large a part of the earth. Never had so many nations been involved. Never had the slaughter been so comprehensive and indiscriminate."—1962, pp. 1, 2.

Even if you were not living at the time of World War I to appreciate the impact it had, you still have witnessed the fulfillment of Jesus' prophecy. For, as Professor H. S. Commager of Amherst College said:

> "[World War I] ushered in a half century of conflict—turbulence, war, revolution, desolation, and ruin on a scale never before seen or even imagined." —*The Saturday Review,* November 9, 1968.

World War II dwarfed the first world war, being four times as costly in lives and in destruction. And the prophetic "great sword" has not been sheathed since then. In 1967, *U.S. News & World Report* said:

> "Is the world in greater tumult than before World War II? No doubt.
>
> "*Shooting troubles,* on the average, erupt *once a month.* Counting out real wars like Korea and Vietnam, the record still shows *over 300* revolutions, coups, uprisings, rebellions and insurrections worldwide since the end of World War II."[42]

Human predictions of peace have failed. The expressed hope of world leaders that World War I would "make the world safe for democracy" and be "a war to end all wars" proved fruitless. Equally fruitless was their prediction that World War II would introduce 'freedom of worship and speech, freedom from fear and want—for all men, everywhere.' Yet, Jesus' prophecy accurately described this warring world's destructive course. Does this not give sound reason for believing that his promise of approaching "deliverance" will also prove true?

DESPITE SCIENTIFIC ADVANCEMENT, AN ERA OF FOOD SHORTAGES

However, world war was only part of the prophetic "sign" that would mark the time when Jesus Christ would take his Kingdom power in heaven. Following the symbolic rider with the "great sword" Jesus foretold that there would be another rider, one representing food shortages. (Revelation 6:5, 6) In the parallel prophecy at Matthew 24:7 Jesus warned:

> "There will be food shortages . . . in one place after another."

Have you not seen this prophecy fulfilled? Horrible famines ravaged many countries after World War I. But you did not have to be living then to bear witness to the prophecy's accuracy. You have likely read reports in your newspaper or seen pictures on television testifying to the gravity of the food crisis right now. The New York *Times* of December 29, 1967, reported:

> "Every 8.6 seconds someone in an underdeveloped country dies as a result of illness caused by malnutrition. . . . 10,000 every day. Over 3,500,000 every year."

But has not hunger been a frequent feature of human history down through the ages? Yes, but modern food shortages are, in many respects, a paradox. For one thing, the food crisis since 1914 has come in spite of major scientific advancements in agriculture. Planting and harvesting techniques have been improved and mechanized. Yet, despite a bounty of crops in many areas, the food crisis is real. As Professor Commager observes:

> "At the end of a generation of unparalleled advance in science and technology, mankind found hunger more widespread, violence more ruthless, and life more insecure than at any time in the century."

A further unusual aspect is that modern food experts see no solution to the problem. Stanford University biologist Dr. Paul Ehrlich in his 1968 book *The Population Bomb* frankly states:

> "The battle to feed all of humanity is over. In the 1970's the world will undergo famines—hundreds of millions of people are going to starve to death in spite of any crash programs embarked upon now. At this late date nothing can prevent a substantial increase in the world death rate." —Prologue.

Only the precision with which Jesus' words have proved true gives hope of coming relief, not by human science, but by God's Kingdom rule over earth.

PESTILENCE AND DISEASE, DESPITE MODERN MEDICINE

We live today in an age of medical marvels. Yet, the prophetic vision given by Jesus showed that still another symbolic horseman, one representing death, would also ride through the earth. Some of his victims would be taken by "deadly plague." (Revelation 6:7, 8) Similarly, as recorded at Luke 21:11, Jesus foretold that there would be:

> " . . . in one place after another pestilences."

Have we seen this fulfilled? Very probably some relatives of yours were laid low by the pestilence that broke out in the autumn of 1918, the Spanish influenza epidemic. It came without warning, killed suddenly, spread to one place after another around the earth. How did it compare with earlier plagues in history? Consider this report in *The Saturday Evening Post* of September 26, 1959:

> "No recorded pestilence before or since has equaled the 1918-1919 death toll in total numbers. In those two years an estimated 21,000,000 died of influenza-pneumonia throughout the world, some 850,000 in the United States alone."

Twentieth-century medicine made little headway against this pestilence. From the equatorial to the Arctic regions, more lives were lost in this flu epidemic than in the four years of battle in World War I. In all the earth, only the islands of St. Helena and Mauritius escaped its ravages!

In spite of further medical progress, disease and pestilence continue to rage throughout the earth. Though the diseases may differ, the so-called "advanced" nations have been hit as well as the "underdeveloped" ones. How many people do you know who have been afflicted by cancer? How many who have suffered from heart disease? According to a 1965 publication of the American Medical Association, lung cancer in the United States was extremely rare in 1900. It "has increased more than 90 per cent since about 1930." Because the heart ailment known as arterial atherosclerosis has afflicted so many persons, the same publication refers to it as "the epidemic of the twentieth century."[43]

Disease factors that have taken on greater proportions than ever before in human history involve pollution—of water, land and air. Concerning this the book *Science & Survival*, by Barry Commoner, says:

> "As a biologist, I have reached this conclusion: we have come to a turning point in the human habitation of the earth. . . . I believe that continued pollution of the earth, if unchecked, will eventually destroy the fitness of this planet as a place for human life."—1966, p. 122.

'GREAT EARTHQUAKES —IN ONE PLACE AFTER ANOTHER'

Yet another outstanding feature of the "sign" given by Jesus is recorded at Matthew 24:7, Mark 13:8 and Luke 21:10, 11. What? "Earthquakes in one place after another," "great earthquakes." Since 1914 have we seen a fulfillment of this feature? Consider the evidence:

In 1915 the quake at Avezzano, Italy, took a toll of 29,970 lives, a quake that hit China in 1920 led to the loss of 180,000 lives; 143,000 persons died as a result of the 1923 quake in Tokyo-

Yokohama, Japan; and 60,000 perished in the 1935 quake in Quetta, India.

But someone may ask, "Have there not always been earthquakes of similar intensity?" Based on data from the United States Coast and Geodetic Survey, a list of major earthquakes in the 1969 *World Almanac* shows 16 major earthquakes during the 200 years prior to 1914. But already in little more than a half century since 1914 there have been nearly *twice* that many major quakes. Pointing to something unusual, the magazine *Scientific American* of September 1950 reported on four periods of earthquakes, separated by quiet intervals, occurring between 1917 and 1948, and then added:

> "But the periods of activity became progressively shorter and closer together. Since 1948 the pattern has entered a new phase, with approximately one great quake a year."

Just in the decade of the 1960's Iran, Chile, Morocco, Yugoslavia, Libya, El Salvador, Russia, Colombia, France, Indonesia, Turkey, Venezuela, Sicily and other lands were hit by great quakes. The upsurge in earthquake activity "in one place after another" since World War I certainly fits the prophecy. This feature of the "sign" is something you are aware of, no matter in what part of the earth you live.

ALL TO BE FULFILLED IN THIS GENERATION

Grim though these facts are, they all add up to proof of the truthfulness of Bible prophecy. These foretold events and conditions may be compared to the pieces of a jigsaw puzzle. Any one of them individually would not make up the "sign" of the "last days." But put together, with *all* of them coming concurrently on the scale Jesus indicated, they make up a complete picture, a vivid one.

Jesus himself used an illustration to help us understand his great prophecy and how it would be fulfilled within the life-span of the generation that saw the fulfillment begin. He said:

> "Note the fig tree and all the other trees: When they are already in the bud, by observing it you know for yourselves that now the summer is near. In this way you also, when you see these things occurring, know that the kingdom of God is near. Truly I say to you, This generation will by no means pass away until all things occur."—Luke 21:29-32.

If we see one tree put out its leaves in mid-winter because the weather is warm for a few days, we do not reason that summer has come, do we? But when we see *all* the trees budding, as well as the days growing longer, and the sun climbing higher into the sky, we know that summer has to be near. Likewise when you see *all* the things that Jesus foretold taking place, you have strong reason to place faith in the Bible as God's Word and know for sure that deliverance is at hand.

But there are yet other outstanding features that fit into the complete pattern of the "sign." They give added meaning to the events and conditions that you are seeing. They accurately describe distinctive attitudes of people in our time.

A CLIMATE OF FEAR

Jesus foretold that the generation that would be living at the time when his kingdom would take power would be exceptionally marked by fear and a sense of foreboding. He said that men would become "faint out of fear and expectation of the things coming upon the inhabited earth." —Luke 21:25, 26.

Would you say that those words describe the generation of this past half century? Has any generation been given greater cause for fear? For the first time in human history world leaders talk with all seriousness of the possibility of the extinction of the human race, by means of modern weaponry. You have watched on television as rockets and manned space capsules are launched into outer space. At the same time news reports show that such rockets are being armed with multiple nuclear heads, capable of spewing out destruction over large areas. Even the moon figures in the maneuvers of political power struggles, concern being expressed that it not be used as a military base. The seas also threaten in a new way. Nuclear-powered submarines prowl its waters, capable of sending nuclear-tipped missiles roaring up and streaking toward major cities, even those located in the middle of continents.

Have verbal and paper agreements of political governments given true relief from this anxiety? To the contrary, people throughout the earth feel as if they are locked into a situation that keeps moving relentlessly toward mass violence. Neither they nor their leaders see any way out, any means of exit from the overall crisis that daily becomes more complex and more explosive. An editorial from *The Saturday Review* recently described the global scene in this way:

"Throughout the entire world people are caught up in convulsive change. The old historical rhythms are hardly recognizable. Issues that formerly took a century or more to come to a boil are in constant eruption. Everything is being bunched up—time, space, nations, people, issues. And everything has a fuse attached to it."—June 22, 1968.

People may seek to shut these world problems out of their minds. Nevertheless, the fears of this generation are becoming more and more personal, reaching ever closer to home. How so?

INCREASING LAWLESSNESS AND LOSS OF LOVE

Jesus' prophecy also foretold an "increasing of lawlessness." (Matthew 24:12) You have seen this fulfilled, and perhaps personally felt its effects. Not merely some temporary, local outbreak of crime but, as the New York *Times* of June 6, 1968, put it:

> "A plague of lawlessness and violence . . . is now sweeping the globe."

There are those who would say, "Oh, it's only the population growth and better reporting methods that make lawlessness seem worse." But the following news report shows otherwise:

> "Washington, May 31 (AP)—FBI Director J. Edgar Hoover assailed today those who attempt to minimize the nation's crime problem by blaming it on the large increase in the youthful population and fuller tabulations by police. . . . He said those who try to 'explain away the shocking truth behind crime statistics' are doomed to failure."[44]

The extent of the "shocking truth" of this "increasing of lawlessness" is spelled out in *U.S. News & World Report* of June 3, 1968:

> "Families find their neighborhoods are becoming unsafe for children or adults. Merchants complain of inadequate police protection for their employes and property in the cities. Citizens are afraid to walk the streets, or to travel by public transportation. Public parks become hangouts for hoodlums . . . Suburbanites fear to venture into the downtown areas for shopping or the theater. Tourists shun the historic shrines once visited in the cities."

And showing that this situation is the result of disregard for law that is affecting the entire globe, the same publication states:

"A climax of some kind seems to be approaching the world over, in resistance to all authority, in tolerated violence, crime, undisciplined behavior."

Note that Jesus' prophecy also foretold that "because of the increasing of lawlessness the love of the greater number will cool off." (Matthew 24:12) Have you not discerned a marked change in people's attitude toward their fellowmen? Where once there was willingness to stop and help a person in trouble, now many prefer to turn away—for fear of lawless attack.

And what of people's attitude toward God? Have you not observed that the conduct of the vast majority of professed Christians reflects a 'cooling off' in their love for God? Note the following reports:

"For every third German in the Federal Republic, God is dead."—*Der Spiegel,* December 18, 1967.

"The majority of the Danish people live without God."—Dean Nepper-Christensen, *Kristeligt Dagblad,* September 26, 1963.

"God has been dethroned; sex has been deified." —Brisbane, Australia, *Courier-Mail,* June 15, 1964.

"The working classes have almost abandoned the church in England, France and Germany. The areas of man's everyday life in our culture have become more and more secular, organized without any reference to God."—Toronto *Daily Star,* January 2, 1960.

Jesus' apostle Paul also gave prophetic warning that such attitudes would mark the "last days." At 2 Timothy 3:1-12 he said:

"In the last days critical times hard to deal with will be here. For men will be lovers of themselves, lovers of money, . . . disobedient to parents, unthankful, . . . not open to any agreement, . . . headstrong, puffed up with pride, lovers of pleasures rather than lovers of God, having a form of godly devotion but proving false to its power."

Do you not see these very conditions in your daily experiences? So many persons think only of their own interests; so many make money their chief aim in life. Juvenile delinquency assumes frightening proportions, following the pattern of adult misbehavior and disregard for authority. Men talk, talk, talk, while strikes and disputes of all kinds demonstrate that, as prophesied, people are "not open to any agreement." The love of pleasure reduces the "godly devotion" of millions into a mere "form," lacking any power to direct or motivate their lives.

It is not only the extent of modern immorality that is outstanding. As philosopher Will Herberg observed:

"The moral crisis of our time consists primarily not in the widespread violation of accepted moral standards—when has any age been free of that? —but in the repudiation of those very moral standards themselves. . . . It is here that we find a breakdown in morality in a radical sense."[45]

This strong trend toward breaking down and doing away with all moral standards is notably characteristic of this generation, even as the Bible prophecies forewarned.

WHAT THE FULFILLMENT OF THESE PROPHECIES MEANS

You have seen the things here discussed. They are not just isolated happenings, nor are they passing, momentary situations. Since the year 1914,* the year that historians now recognize as

* For evidence that Bible chronology pointed to the year 1914, see the book *From Paradise Lost to Paradise Regained,* page 173.

"the turning point in our time," the evidence has steadily piled up, year upon year, for more than half a century. While human predictions of global peace and prosperity have regularly failed, the worsening world conditions have consistently demonstrated the amazing precision of the Bible prophecies. Is not this powerful evidence that the Bible is not a book of mere human origin? Surely only God could foresee with such accuracy the course that men and nations would take, yes, even the trembling movements within this planet, many centuries beforehand.

To the majority, these events and conditions are puzzling. The Bible prophecies, however, give them meaning; they explain how they all fit together to form a global "sign." This "sign" can be seen and read by anyone, anywhere on earth, if that person is willing to examine it in the light of Bible prophecy. The many parts of the prophetic "sign" combine to show that this generation is living in the "last days" of the present unrighteous systems. They point to an approaching world change, a change brought about by God's power, operating through the Kingdom government of his Son Christ Jesus. (Luke 21:31; Daniel 2:44; 7:13, 14) So, the "sign" speaks of the need for prompt action now, if we want to receive God's promised blessings and not be found in a course that makes us objects of his wrath.—Luke 21:34-36; 2 Peter 3:13, 14.

These Bible prophecies provide the one reliable source of hope in this time of mankind's greatest crisis. They alone give sound reason to "lift your heads up, because your deliverance is getting near." Does not this demonstrate that the Bible is indeed a book for our day?

CHAPTER 11

Is the Bible Practical for Our Day?

WE WOULD expect a book that is the Word of God to be the most practical book in the world. Its teachings, when put to the test, ought to work. People who put its counsel into practice in their lives should see results. And these results should be, not merely good, but superior to those obtainable by any other means. If this proves true with the Bible, it should certainly be convincing evidence that the Bible is God's guide for man, a 'lamp to one's foot and a light to one's roadway.'—Psalm 119:105.

Just what will applying the Bible's counsel do for a person now, in the present time? Will the poor man thereby become rich? Will the sick person gain perfect health? And will the life of any man or woman, or even a family, become free of all problems?

No, the Bible does not say that will happen within the present framework of conditions. The Bible is not a book of philosophy that refuses to face the facts of life. Of all books, it most honestly states those facts as they are and shows why problems are a part of present living in human imperfection. Yet, of all books, it alone sets forth guiding principles for handling both the major problems and the minor ones that arise in every feature of human living. So, it offers improvement and happiness *now,* plus a grand hope for the future. And it offers this for people of every race, nationality and circumstance. Consider its counsel in some vital areas of life.

REMEDYING ECONOMIC PROBLEMS

Poverty is a major problem in large sectors of the earth. Can the Bible put more bread on a man's table? Yes, it can, if being a more conscientious, more energetic worker will do it. The Bible encourages industry and shows why laziness is detestable in God's sight. (Proverbs 6: 6-11; 10:26; 2 Thessalonians 3:10-12) It can free a man from the chains of superstitious traditions that often hamper learning and progress. (Isaiah 44:14-20; Mark 7:6-8; John 8:32) It can save him money by giving him a new set of values, and by exposing the folly of looking to luck and fortune in gambling. (1 Timothy 6:6-12; Isaiah 65:11) Other costly habits may be weeded out by following the Bible's counsel on keeping free from defiling practices. (2 Corinthians 7:1) A person is protected against poverty due to drunkenness by adhering to what the Bible says about moderation. (Proverbs 23:29, 30) The man who puts Bible counsel to work in his life no longer lets his strength be eaten up by the acid of bitter resentment or envy. (Psalm 37:1-5) And even though injustices or discrimination may exist, is it not the man with an established reputation as an honest, diligent, reliable worker who is eventually preferred over the one who is not? —Proverbs 10:4; 12:24.

It is an acknowledged fact that a workingman's mental attitude is a major factor in success.

Tiredness, accidents and many other undesirable things can come from a poor mental attitude. The Bible, then, is very practical in coming to the aid of the worker who follows its counsel, giving him a good outlook and the assurance of a reward better than his pay envelope. By applying this counsel, even slaves in the ancient Roman Empire could work, not as men pleasers, but sincerely, "whole-souled as to Jehovah, and not to men, for you know that it is from Jehovah you will receive the due reward of the inheritance."—Colossians 3:22-25; see also Ephesians 6:5-9.

IMPROVED MENTAL AND PHYSICAL HEALTH

Despite modern medical science, health continues to be one of life's major problems. Can the Bible contribute toward improved health? Yes, because there are certain health factors that apply equally to all. One is the effect of the mental attitude and the emotions on the body. This effect is referred to many times in the Bible. For instance, Proverbs 14:30 says: "A calm heart is the life of the fleshly organism, but jealousy is rottenness to the bones." Now, thousands of years later, the 1956 edition of *The Encyclopedia Americana* (Vol. 18, p. 582b) states:

> "Since 1940 it has become more and more apparent that the physiologic function of organs and the organs systems are closely allied to the state of mind of the individual and that even tissue changes may occur in an organ so affected."

A book published by the American Medical Association states:

> "It is estimated that 50 to 70 per cent of the patients going to a family doctor suffer from an illness of an emotional rather than a physical nature."[46]

Showing how emotions affect bodily health, Dr. J. E. Hett in his book *Cancer* says:

> "The impulses of shock, worry, hatred, anger, jealousy, revenge and ill-will put extra pressure upon the endocrine glands. Through these the functions of the stomach and intestines are inhibited. Poisons are created which do damage to the tissues. These, in turn, interfere with the proper activity of the mind. It becomes a vicious circle." —P. 85.

The Bible directs persons away from damaging emotions and attitudes. It counsels: "Let all malicious bitterness and anger and wrath and screaming and abusive speech be taken away from you along with all injuriousness. But become kind to one another, tenderly compassionate." (Ephesians 4:31, 32) It aids one to manifest the fruitage of God's spirit, which is "love, joy, peace, long-suffering, kindness, goodness, faith, mildness, self-control."—Galatians 5:22, 23.

The healthful effect of replacing negative, damaging emotions with positive, upbuilding qualities is clear. But some object that this is "easier said than done." True, most worthwhile things are. But this does not make them impractical. The Bible makes such a change possible. How? By providing healthful food on which one's mind and heart can feed for a lifetime.—Proverbs 3:7, 8; 4:20-22; Philippians 4:8.

The Bible teaches obedience to God and to laws of man that do not conflict with God's laws. This is of great value to a person, for it protects him from becoming involved in crimes, riots and other wrongdoing. He has a good conscience, which is a blessing that contributes much toward maintaining good physical health and a happy disposition.—1 Peter 3:16-18.

Not only this, but the Bible's high standards of cleanness and morality protect against many loathsome diseases. (Proverbs 7:5, 22-27) The Bible's exhortation to moderation in eating and drinking likewise promotes better health. (Proverbs 23:20; Luke 21:34) As an article on "Longevity" by Sir Humphry Rolleston, M.D., and statistician Alfred J. Lotka says of persons living to an age of a hundred or more:

> "The majority . . . have been small eaters, . . . Overfeeding by overworking the resources of the body leads to metabolic disease, such as diabetes . . . arterial, heart and kidney [ailments], . . . With regard to the influence of alcohol there can be no doubt, as the actuarial reports of life assurance companies amply prove, that excess is harmful."[47]

In all these respects, then, the Bible's counsel is practical. It can add years to one's life.

But what about its moral requirements? Have not present conditions forced a reevaluation of the Bible's moral code?

MORALITY AND MARRIAGE

Many today are rejecting the Bible's moral standards. But why? Is it because they are impractical? Or is it an excuse for loose conduct?

Does one "miss out on something" by holding to Bible standards? Note this comment by Maurice Zolotow:

> "For about fifteen years I have been the confidant of Broadway and Hollywood actors and actresses who have opportunities to live a promiscuous sexual life. And some of them live it to the hilt . . . But when they trust you and let down their hair, they will confess how frustrating and unsatisfying it all is."[48]

A few minutes of illicit sexual excitement, or having a clean conscience with self-respect twenty-four hours a day, year in and year out—which makes more sense? Which can bring genuine satisfaction and happiness? How undeniably practical the Bible's counsel is when it says:

> "For as a honeycomb the lips of a strange woman keep dripping . . . But the aftereffect from her is as bitter as wormwood . . . do not get near to the entrance of her house, that you may not give to others your dignity, . . . [nor] have to groan in your future when your flesh and your organism come to an end. . . . rejoice with the wife of your youth."—Proverbs 5:3-11, 18.

The Bible expresses Jehovah God's condemnation of the man who deals treacherously with his wife "although she is your partner." (Malachi 2:14-16) Marriage is the most intimate of all partnerships. In any other partnership, such as a commercial one, is it practical to cheat on your partner, slyly divert your time and effort to outside interests, even to those of a competitor? How rewarding would such a partnership be? On the other hand, the man or woman who rejects immorality and honors the marital relationship can draw to the full on the love, devotion and trust of his or her mate. What this brings in the way of loyal support and cooperation can be a tremendous asset in life.

What has been the result of downgrading the Bible's standards? Today divorce rates spiral upward in many lands. Showing the effects, the magazine *Medical World News* of January 19, 1968, says:

> "The figures [of a California census study] indicate that the population's health problems—general illness, alcoholism, mental illness, and maternal health difficulties—are measurably affected by marital status, with divorce and separation as major factors of attrition."

Each divorce does harm, particularly to any children involved. Each divorce represents a failure, not a success. Is it not practical, then, to apply Bible counsel and safeguard the marital relationship?—Matthew 19:4-9; Hebrews 13:4.

Marital fidelity, of course, is only part of a successful marriage. By practical counsel and examples, the Bible shows how to cope with other problems of family life.

A HAPPY HOMELIFE

The Creator of marriage and of the family should know best how these work to produce genuine happiness. We should expect His Word to give the most practical guidelines for a happy homelife. Consider the following:

Can any family function smoothly if its members are not sure what their respective positions, duties and privileges are? Yet, today there is growing uncertainty about these. This is especially true in the matter of headship. In some parts of the world the headship of the husband is not merely undisputed; it is often harsh and dictatorial, making the lot of the wife an unhappy one. In other parts, there is a growing tendency for the wife to challenge or even reject the husband's headship, and in such areas the divorce rate is high.

The Bible favors neither of these extremes. While it unmistakably assigns headship to the husband, it shows that the wife shares a privileged standing with him before God. As Professor Woody observes in the *Encyclopædia Britannica:* "Hebraic-Christian ethics elevated woman morally."[49] She is assigned "honor as to a weaker vessel, the feminine one," and a good and capable wife is described as a "crown" to her husband, having value "far more than that of corals," worthy of her husband's praise. (1 Peter 3:7; Proverbs 12:4; 31:10, 28) Still the Bible holds firmly to the principle of husbandly headship. Is this really practical?

More and more, scientific evidence points to the distinction between man and woman, as long ago set forth in the Bible. Biologists say they can take a single cell from a person and from it determine that person's sex. Not only the man's part in procreation and his more rugged build, but also the hormones his body produces show he is meant to be the more aggressive of the sexes and to take the lead. Young children reflect their future roles in life even in the playthings they select. While intelligence in man and woman is approximately the same, there are basic emotional differences that fit them for their respective roles. As a result of research done for the National Management Association, psychologist Cleo Dawson points out:

> " . . . basically, women *feel* while men *think*. Women frequently measure up to men and surpass them in intelligence, but they are handicapped by the weight of emotional drag. Men have more practical minds; they can judge, organize, direct. Thus the supervision of women by men seems to be nature's plan, however desperately women may fight it."[50]

Accurately, then, the Bible sets out the basic formula for marital happiness in these words:

> "Let wives be in subjection to their husbands as to the Lord . . . Husbands ought to be loving their wives as their own bodies. . . . for no man ever hated his own flesh; but he feeds and cherishes it, . . . on the other hand, the wife should have deep respect for her husband."—Ephesians 5:22-33.

No matter what the overtones or undertones, cannot most difficulties in the husband-wife relationship be improved by attention to these two things: the husband's manifesting affection and the wife's showing respect?

Juvenile delinquency is another major problem of modern times. Along with it we see an increase in parental permissiveness, relaxing of supervision. The Bible warns that a child "let on the loose" causes shame, that "foolishness is tied up with the heart of a boy; the rod of discipline is what will remove it far from him." (Proverbs 29:15; 22:15) But will just continual strictness or physical chastisement correct matters? No, and so parents are counseled:

> "You fathers, do not be exasperating your children, so that they do not become downhearted." —Colossians 3:21.

Though parents, like their children, are imperfect, to the extent that they develop a blend of firmness and affection they can enjoy the respect and love of their offspring.

Today family ties are cracking under the pressures and stresses of modern conditions. Sharing the same dwelling and being of the same blood relationship are not holding families together. What can the Bible do for the family unit to give it the strength it needs? This: it can bind the members together by the sense of responsibility and loyalty that it produces toward One greater than any member of the family.

Through the Bible's teachings each family member is helped to appreciate that he is answerable to the heavenly Life-giver for things said and done. This gives weight to the father's counsel or discipline, as well as to the mother's teaching of the children. It helps the husband to shoulder his responsibility, aids the wife to find greater pleasure in her work, reminds the children that their parents too receive godly discipline. (Hebrews 12:8-11) Each member feels the desire to make a determined effort so that the family life will bring honor, not discredit, to Jehovah.

Further proof of the Bible's practicality is that it provides for the eventuality of divided families. Jesus Christ frankly stated that the truths he spoke would act as a "sword" in some families, one or more members accepting, the others rejecting. (Matthew 10:34-37) The Bible gives comfort and wise counsel even in such cases. (1 Corinthians 7:12-16; 1 Peter 3:1-6) And the love it teaches, which "does not look for its own interests, does not become provoked . . . does not keep account of the injury," but which "bears all things, . . . hopes all things, endures all things," makes it possible to find happiness even in these trying circumstances.—1 Corinthians 13:4-7.

ENJOYING PEACEFUL RELATIONSHIPS AND SECURITY

Life is not all spent in the home. And though it is not hard to get along with those outside it who are friendly, pleasant and considerate (Matthew 5:46, 47), unfortunately many are just not that way today. What will you do when someone acts discourteously, speaks harsh words, or discriminates against you?

The Bible's counsel is: "He that is slow to anger is better than a mighty man, and he that is controlling his spirit than the one capturing a city." (Proverbs 16:32) Is this practical? In Paris, France, when a man carrying a case passed close to a new car, the driver jumped out, accused him of scratching the car and struck him such a severe blow that the man never regained consciousness. Such explosions of anger are typical of the present high-speed age in which we live. But are they practical?

It is true that in many places a "dog-eat-dog" attitude prevails. But how much happiness can an intelligent human find in acting like a dog? To those suffering injustices the Bible supplies comfort and moral strength for holding to high standards of conduct. It says:

> "Return evil for evil to no one. . . . If possible, as far as it depends upon you, be peaceable with all men. Do not avenge yourselves, beloved, but yield place to the wrath; for it is written: 'Vengeance is mine; I will repay, says Jehovah.' But, 'if your enemy is hungry, feed him; if he is thirsty, give him something to drink; for by doing this you will heap fiery coals upon his head.' Do not let yourself be conquered by the evil, but keep conquering the evil with the good."—Romans 12:17-21.

Some call this "idealistic" and say "realism" requires another attitude in this modern time. "What would happen if most of the people in a country adopted such an attitude?" they ask. "What security would there be?" Well, what is happening today with the majority showing an *opposite* attitude? Has this brought security to mankind? Has it brought security to you as an individual?

Would you feel secure living in a neighborhood where all homes were surrounded by electrically charged fences, the lawns sown with land mines, the porches having mounted machine guns? Though the picture may seem extreme, this is the direction in which mankind, divided by distrust, fears and prejudices, is heading. Can you change this trend? No, and the Bible does not ask you to try. It shows that only God can and will do so. Plainly, no solution or search for security that leaves Him out can be truly practical. —Psalm 37:8-11.

In an earlier chapter, we have seen that Bible prophecies foretold this time of man's greatest extremity, the time when so many plans and inventions of men who do not look to the Bible for guidance are proving unworkable or just plain deadly. Reasonably we should expect the Bible to show us what we need to do in this time of greatest danger. It does.

Far from telling us to do nothing, the Bible shows the need for urgent action now. Action, not in a lost cause, but in a cause directed by divine wisdom, a cause certain of success. First, it calls on us to educate ourselves in the principles and teachings of the Bible, learning to apply them in our daily life. Then, it leads us to unite with God's people world wide in helping still others to do the same. (Revelation 22:17) All this is in preparation for survival and for gaining eternal life, not on some other planet, but right here on earth in a new order of God's making. Is this reasonable? Well, have you not read and heard statements time and again by prominent men and world rulers warning that *man* may destroy *all* life on earth? Then why should it seem strange for God to intervene and destroy all unrighteous persons from off the earth while preserving the righteous ones? In view of this, the Bible counsel on godly conduct is, indeed, practical wisdom.—Psalm 37:9; 2 Peter 2:9.

LIVING PROOF OF THE BIBLE'S PRACTICALITY

The points here considered are not just theory. There is living proof of their practicality. Consider these statements made by outsiders regarding a certain Bible-based society of Christians:

The New York *Times* reported on a 1958 international convention of this society, attended by persons from 123 different lands. These people represented all branches of the human family. Yet the report observed:

> "New York has been host for the last six days to its biggest and in all likelihood its best-behaved convention.
>
> "Since Sunday some 180,000 Jehovah's Witnesses have been eating, sleeping and working in the metropolitan area. . . .
>
> "New Yorkers . . . are unanimous in agreeing that the Witnesses' conduct has been exemplary. . . . Their cleanliness is now almost legendary." —August 1, 1958.

Showing the practicality of their attitudes and organization is a report by *Life* magazine on the same convention. It said:

> "Some 35,000 delegates came from overseas. The special transportation included two chartered ships, eight trains, 65 planes, 500 buses and 18,000 auto pools. Everything ran so smoothly that even blasé New Yorkers were impressed."—August 11, 1958.

Of this same society, the Italian magazine *Selezione Piacentina* said in 1968:

> "They have such courteous manners and purity of mind . . . people marvelously simple and happy, free and thoroughly committed to the study of the Word of God as written in the Bible. . . . Their morals, like their faith, do not know of any breaches, subterfuges, half measures, hypocritical camouflage."

The book *Christians of the Copperbelt* includes a report on African members of this society in the Copperbelt region, Zambia. Regarding their dependability and behavior, this comment is made:

"African teachers and welfare workers whose education enables them to have a more detached point of view said, 'Watchtower [Jehovah's witnesses] are very reliable people and punctual. They have good discipline and do not drink too much.' . . . We found them surprisingly contrasting in this respect with most other groups."—1961, p. 231.

Regarding family relationships, the same book shows how Bible teachings changed long-standing customs and traditions:

"The [African] Watchtower families we learnt to know seem to be exceptionally well-adjusted and happy together.

"This attitude of man and woman working together in their family units was very obvious in the homes . . . While it was rather difficult in most other congregations to find out who was married to whom, because husbands and wives neither came to the church together nor sat together during the service, the Watchtower families were easily recognized in their meetings as little clusters of father, mother and children."—Pp. 235, 112.

Though persecuted in many lands, this society has increased in numbers throughout the years. Speaking of the experiences of these Christians in Nazi concentration camps, Björn Hallström, well-known Swedish journalist, said:

"They were treated worse than any other group, but they managed, through their belief in God, to survive better than any others."

Professor of Educational Psychology Bruno Bettelheim, who served terms of imprisonment in Dachau and Buchenwald Nazi concentration camps, also writes of these Christians and indicates why they were able to survive. In his book *The Informed Heart*, he says:

"[Jehovah's witnesses] not only showed unusual heights of human dignity and moral behavior, but seemed protected against the same camp experience that soon destroyed persons considered very well integrated by my psychoanalytic friends and myself.

"They were even less affected by imprisonment, and kept their integrity, thanks to rigid religious beliefs.

"Because of their conscientious work habits they were often selected as foremen. . . . Even though they were the only group of prisoners who never abused or mistreated other prisoners, . . . SS officers preferred them as orderlies because of their work habits, skills, or unassuming attitudes. Quite in contrast to the continuous internecine warfare among the other prisoners groups, the Jehovah's Witnesses never misused their closeness to the SS officers to gain positions of privilege in the camp." —1961, pp. 20, 21, 122, 123.

There is, then, evidence throughout the earth that the Bible's counsel works in our day. If a thousand, a hundred thousand, yes, hundreds of thousands of persons have found that they can change their lives to measure up to Bible standards, with excellent results, can anyone rightly say the Bible is not practical? The words written by the apostle Paul to fellow Christians in his day apply to these persons in our day:

"We also thank God incessantly, because when you received God's word, which you heard from us, you accepted it, not as the word of men, but, just as it truthfully is, as the word of God, which is also *at work in you believers*."—1 Thessalonians 2:13.

The Bible invites you to put its teachings to the test in *your* life. Thereby you may prove for yourself that these teachings are, not theories or philosophies of men, but part of the Word of the living God.—Psalm 34:8; Malachi 3:10; Matthew 6:31-33.

CHAPTER 12

How the Bible Came to Us

THE evidence all points to the conclusion that the Bible is indeed God's Word. But how did the Bible come to us? Did God write it and then hand it to man? If he used men to write it, how can we say it is God's? Did God tell them just what words to write? If he did not always dictate it to them, then how do we know that the writers did not make mistakes or simply put down their own ideas?

For the answers to these questions, we need to examine what the Bible means when it says that it is "inspired of God."

HOW WAS IT INSPIRED?

Even persons who think the Bible to be nothing more than a good book have said it is inspired. But in what way? They mean in the same way that poets and musicians are said to be inspired. They think of a Bible writer, say Isaiah or David, as being like a talented poet, completely carried away by some grand theme, so that, as it is said, he is "inspired" to produce a masterpiece.

This means that they look upon the Bible as a collection of books written by devout men, rather than as a work written under the direction of a single, divine Author, through the operation of his holy spirit or invisible active force. The latter view is what the Bible itself claims, saying that "all Scripture is inspired of God," and that "prophecy was at no time brought by man's will, but men spoke from God as they were borne along by holy spirit."—2 Timothy 3:16; 2 Peter 1:21.

The expression "inspired of God" is translated from a Greek word meaning "God-breathed." By 'breathing' his own spirit upon faithful men, God moved them to write the Sacred Scriptures. This means that God implanted messages or visions in the circuits of their receptive minds. It was then the prophets' responsibility to write these down.—2 Samuel 23:2; Revelation 1:19.

Early in the Bible's writing, "God's finger" inscribed the Ten Commandments on stone tablets. (Exodus 31:18) These commandments are the only part of the Bible that God personally recorded by the direct action of his spirit on the tablets. In writing all other parts of the Bible, he used humans as his penmen or secretaries.

At times God dictated messages or conveyed them by angelic messengers to faithful men, and these wrote the messages down exactly as given. (Exodus 34:27; Isaiah 56:1; Jeremiah 11:1) Moses received many messages dictated by God, and he recorded them faithfully. In fact, when Moses received God's law at Mount Sinai, God stated to him: "These are the words that you are to say to the sons of Israel." But what proof did others have that God was dealing with Moses? God performed signs so that the people would recognize that He was really using Moses as His spokesman on earth. At Mount Sinai, God caused thunders and lightnings, "and a heavy cloud upon the mountain and a very loud sound of a horn, so that all the people who were in the camp began to tremble." The millions that witnessed this display had convincing proof that God was speaking to them through Moses.—Exodus 19:3-25.

Centuries later, when he formed the Christian congregation, God again demonstrated with supernatural signs, seen by people from many nations, that his spirit was on that congregation's members. He used certain ones of these men to record the Christian Greek Scriptures. As the Bible points out, "God joined in bearing witness with signs as well as portents and various powerful works and with distributions of holy spirit." —Hebrews 2:4; Acts 2:1-43.

It seems evident that in many cases the inspired penmen were allowed to use a certain amount of personal initiative in their style of writing. Though God's spirit guided their thoughts, they made their own choice of words in expressing the divine message. Yet the message remained God's. This principle is illustrated by practices in our day. The manager of a business firm may instruct his secretary to answer a letter, stating the points to be made. The secretary writes the letter, guided by the instructions and, from experience, knowing to some extent the "mind" of the manager on such matters. The manager reads the letter, approves it as an accurate expression of his thoughts and signs it. It is recognized as a letter from him.—1 Corinthians 2:11-16; 4:1, 2.

Sometimes God's spirit caused a Bible writer to see visions or mental pictures. Thereafter the Bible writer recorded what he had seen.—Ezekiel 1:1; Daniel 7:1; Revelation 1:10, 11; 4:1.

It should not be difficult for us today to understand how the heavenly Creator could cause these Bible writers on earth to see pictures in their minds or to hear a divine voice. A person today can sit in his own home and see on a television screen a picture that originates at a distant point, and that is transmitted by making use of physical laws that the Creator long ago put into operation. Is it, then, too great a thing for God himself to convey to the minds of his servants visions of things to come?

When astronauts orbited the moon, they broadcast messages back to the earth, and these were received with remarkable clarity. Could not God in heaven transmit messages to his servants in a far superior manner? Certainly! Note, too, that only those with the necessary receiving equipment, properly tuned in, could hear what the astronauts said. So, too, God could and did beam his messages to earth to faithful men who were in tune with him and he commanded them to record what they received.

This very unusual method of authorship resulted in a unique masterpiece—a work having one Author but many writers. There is a superb inner harmony that reflects the mastermind of this one Author. The same theme emphasizing God's kingdom runs throughout the whole, from 'paradise lost' in Genesis to 'paradise regained' in Revelation. It took about 1,600 years for at least thirty-nine Bible writers to complete the writing of the Bible. What does this show? It shows that these men could not possibly have 'put their heads together' so as to *make* everything harmonize. There could have been no collusion, for the writers in some cases lived centuries apart. Some of them even testified that they did not understand the significance of things they wrote. (Daniel 12:8, 9; 1 Peter 1:10-12) But the divine Author understood and he is responsible for the Bible's unified message.

A DIVINE LIBRARY

Are you confused when it comes to finding your way around in the Bible? If so, then you know how bewildered the young boy feels when he enters the city library for the first time and is faced with its array of many books. However, with just a little explanation the boy soon learns where to locate things. He begins to appreciate why the books are not on the shelves in the same order in which they were written. He understands why they are not arranged as he might like to have them, with the ones most interesting to him on the first shelf and the least interesting on the last.

This illustration of a library aptly applies to the Bible. The English word "Bible" comes from the Greek word *bi·bli'a,* which in time came to describe various scrolls, books and eventually the *collection* of little books that make up our Bible. Jerome, known for his ancient Latin translation of the Bible, called this collection the "Divine Library."

The first thirty-nine books of the Bible (according to the listing in most modern translations) were written mainly in Hebrew, with very small portions in Aramaic. The last twenty-seven books were written in Greek, the common international language of the people when Jesus Christ was on earth. So it is appropriate to refer to the two major sections of the Bible as the "Hebrew Scriptures" and the "Greek Scriptures."

While the arrangement of the thirty-nine books

of the Hebrew Scriptures may vary somewhat in different versions, they are often grouped into three general sections: (1) *Historic,* Genesis to Esther, seventeen books; (2) *Poetic,* Job to The Song of Solomon, five books; (3) *Prophetic,* Isaiah to Malachi, seventeen books. These, of course, are only general divisions, for in any one section elements of the other two may be found. The twenty-seven books of the Christian Greek Scriptures are also grouped in three logical classes: (1) five historical books, the four Gospels and the Acts; (2) twenty-one letters of certain apostles and disciples; and (3) as a delightful conclusion to the whole Bible, the Revelation with its preview of momentous events of the future.

The more you read the Bible the more you will appreciate the interdependence of its parts. Great changes came with Christianity. Yet the Christian Greek Scriptures merge with the Hebrew Scriptures in a total harmony. The two defy divorce one from the other. The Christian writers expanded on the various themes first set forth in the Hebrew Scriptures. They quoted from them directly more than 365 times, and made about 375 additional references to them. The four Gospels form a climax toward which the prophetic Hebrew Scriptures kept building. The rest of the Christian Greek Scriptures apply and explain much of the Hebrew Scriptures in the light of Christianity. Even the prophecies found in the inspired Greek Scriptures form an extension and expansion of those in the Hebrew Scriptures.

The Bible, then, is in no sense an unrelated assortment of fragments from Jewish and Christian literature. Rather, it is a carefully compiled library of inspired books, all interconnected by a central theme, and preserved for our comfort and encouragement in this day. This grand Book reflects the wisdom and unity of purpose of the Creator-Author himself.

DOES MY BIBLE AGREE WITH THE ORIGINAL?

Many people have asked this question. What are the facts? Because the material on which the Bible books were originally written was perishable, we do not have any of the original writings. But we do have an abundance of *copies* of the originals. In fact, right from the beginning of Bible writing, God authorized the making of copies of the original inspired writings.—Deuteronomy 17:18.

But how do we know that these were copied accurately? Can you be sure that your Bible contains the original Word inspired by God?

On this point, history tells us that the copyists of the Hebrew Scriptures were noted for their painstaking accuracy. Handwritten copies (manuscripts) were very carefully made by special schools of scribes. It is true that their copying was not inspired. But many were God-fearing men like Ezra, who is called "a skilled copyist in the law of Moses, which Jehovah the God of Israel had given." (Ezra 7:6) Of certain later scribes called the Masoretes, it is recorded that their motto was to "change nothing, reproduce everything, fence and guard everything." Evidence of the extreme care exercised can be seen in ancient manuscripts where not only the number of words but even the letters were laboriously counted and noted in the margins, thereby guarding against error or omission.

Someone may say: "Even with such care, surely the copying and recopying of the Scriptures over hundreds and even thousands of years must have resulted in a large number of inaccuracies." Yet, remarkably, this is not the case. Consider, for example, the famous Dead Sea Scrolls. From 1947 to 1955 these manuscripts were found, including copies of books of the Hebrew Scriptures. They date from 100 to 200 B.C.E. One of the scrolls is a copy of the book of Isaiah. Before its discovery, the oldest known Hebrew text of Isaiah was one dating from the tenth century C.E. So this discovery meant that the time previously separating the original writing of Isaiah from its nearest copy was now reduced to about one-half! Yet, when the ancient Dead Sea Scroll of Isaiah was compared with the copy made a thousand years later, only very minor differences appeared, most of them variations in spelling.

Besides this, there are a large number of other ancient manuscripts available so that, by means of comparison, even the few errors that have crept in can be identified and corrected. As the book *The Bible from the Beginning* states:

> "In the number of ancient MSS. [manuscripts] attesting a writing, and in the number of years that had elapsed between the original and the attesting MSS., the Bible enjoys a decided advantage over classical writings [such as those of Homer, Plato and others]. . . . Altogether classical MSS. are but a handful compared with Biblical. No ancient book is so well attested as the Bible."
> —Pp. 74, 76.

There are more than 1,700 ancient manuscripts of the Hebrew Scriptures, the whole or in part, in libraries or museums around the world. The oldest of these dates back to the first or second century B.C.E. There are also thousands of manuscripts of the inspired Greek Scriptures. Many of these date from the third century C.E. The oldest is a papyrus fragment of the Gospel of John. It dates from about 150 C.E. This is only some fifty years after the original was written by John! Thus, as Sir Frederic Kenyon observed:

> "The interval then between the dates of original composition and the earliest extant evidence becomes so small as to be in fact negligible, and the last foundation for any doubt that the Scriptures have come down to us substantially as they were written has now been removed."—*The Bible and Archaeology,* pp. 288, 289.

True, minor differences may appear in the ancient copies. But they are of no consequence as to the message conveyed. As the noted Greek-language authorities Westcott and Hort point out regarding the Christian Greek Scriptures:

> "If comparative trivialities, such as changes of order, the insertion or omission of the article with proper names, and the like, are set aside, the words in our opinion still subject to doubt can hardly amount to more than a thousandth part of the whole New Testament."[51]

Any who say your Bible today lacks evidence of accurate transmission, therefore, are evidently unaware of these well-established facts. Certainly we should expect God to see to it that his Word would be preserved in such a way that the truth, principles and understanding it conveys were protected. The Bible itself contains God's promise to preserve it in this way.—Daniel 12:4; 1 Peter 1:24, 25; Revelation 22:18, 19.

WHY SO MANY DIFFERENT VERSIONS?

If you read ancient Hebrew, Aramaic and Greek, then you have no need for a translation; you can read the Bible in its original languages.

But most of mankind must rely on translations in their own languages. The Bible, or portions of it, is now available in over 1,300 languages.

Also, since language constantly changes, new Bible versions are made in order to keep up with language changes, and for this we should be thankful. For example, note the adjustments made in less than 600 years in three English versions in rendering Matthew 11:12:

> "And fro the daies of Joon Baptist til now the kyngdom of heuenes suffrith violence, and violent men rauyschen it."—Wycliffe-Purvey, c. 1388.
>
> "From the tyme of Jhon baptist hitherto the kyngdom of heven suffreth violence and they that make vyolence pull it vnto them."—Tyndale, 1526.
>
> "But from the days of John the Baptist until now the kingdom of the heavens is the goal toward which men press, and those pressing forward are seizing it."—*New World Translation of the Holy Scriptures*, 1961.

Not only do the later translations make the language more understandable for us today, but they also bring us the benefits of improved knowledge of the ancient languages. Besides this, by making careful comparisons of vast numbers of ancient manuscripts, scholars are able to root out any errors that may have slipped in. An example is the spurious insertion at First John chapter five. The last part of verse 7 and the first part of verse 8 read, according to the *Authorized Version* of 1611 (the Catholic *Douay* version of 1610 reads similarly): "in heaven, the Father, the Word, and the Holy Ghost: and these three are one. And there are three that bear witness in earth." However, for the first thirteen centuries of the Common Era not one single Greek manuscript contains these words. *The Jerusalem Bi-*

ble (Catholic) omits these words altogether, explaining in a footnote that they are "not in any of the early Greek MSS, or any of the early translations." Other translations, both Protestant and Catholic, do likewise.

Thus, modern Bible translations help us to arrive at the correct meaning of what we read.

IS THE BIBLE DIFFICULT FOR YOU TO UNDERSTAND?

The Bible is written in language that is simple and clear, yet forceful and graphic. The actions and events, the prophetic symbols and parables —all are stated in words that can be translated clearly and accurately in most modern-day languages. The Bible is free from the obscure, clouded language characterizing human philosophies. Yet many say they find it difficult to understand. Why? On one occasion Jesus stated:

> "I publicly praise you, Father, Lord of heaven and earth, because you have hidden these things from the wise and intellectual ones and have revealed them to babes. Yes, O Father, because to do thus came to be the way approved by you."—Matthew 11:25, 26.

Does this mean the Bible can only be understood by those who are *not* wise and intellectual? No, for the Bible encourages the gaining of wisdom; Jesus himself was both very wise and intellectual; the apostle Paul was widely known for his great learning. (Proverbs 1:1-7; Matthew 12:42; 13:54; Acts 26:24) What, then, does it mean? It means that those who are wise and intellectual according to worldly standards carry no advantage over those of humble learning and mental development—not when it comes to grasping the real significance and full sense of the Bible's message.—Acts 4:13.

Why is this? It is because "God opposes the haughty ones, but he gives undeserved kindness to the humble ones." (James 4:6) Not all highly educated persons are proud; but this is often the case. Not all persons of little or ordinary education are humble; but many are. Here, then, is further evidence that the Bible is really the Word of God. Clever men can easily write so that only the highly educated will comprehend. But to author a book that more persons of ordinary education will understand than those of greater education—this takes the wisdom of God.—1 Corinthians 1:19, 20, 26-29.

To understand the Bible, then, requires even more of the heart than of the head. It places a premium on sincerity, humility, and love of truth and right. (Proverbs 3:5-7; 28:5; Matthew 18:1-6) Whether one's education is great or little, such understanding calls for earnest effort. A prayerful attitude is also needed.—Psalm 119:34.*

The manner in which the Bible was written and the unified theme it reveals point convincingly to Jehovah God as its Author. The way in which it has been so accurately preserved during thousands of years gives evidence of God's interest in mankind. These are strong reasons for investigating it. They encourage us to 'keep on asking and keep on seeking,' searching for understanding "as for hid treasures." If we do, the Bible assures us, we will find truth and wisdom worth more than gold, silver or costly gems.—Matthew 7:7, 8; Proverbs 2:1-9.

* A clear, straightforward explanation of the basic doctrines and teachings of the Bible may be found in the book *The Truth That Leads to Eternal Life.*

CHAPTER 13

Do Christendom's Churches Represent the Bible?

IN THE minds of many persons the Bible is inseparably linked with Christendom. Christendom refers to those lands and nations where religions claiming to be Christian prevail. If you live in Christendom, it may surprise you to learn that Christendom's history is a major reason why millions in other lands show no interest in the Bible. If you live in a land outside Christendom, you will likely know what we mean.

Wars, oppression, disunity and crime are certainly not what most people are seeking. Yet within Christendom, which claims to represent God, enmity and selfishness have erupted time and again in fierce violence, reaching a peak in the mass slaughter of the two world wars. The second of these conflicts saw a nation of Christendom introduce atomic warfare, dropping atomic bombs on an opposing non-Christian nation.

Crime, of course, can be found in any part of the earth. However, it might be expected that Christendom, supposedly guided by the Word of God, would enjoy a greater freedom from crime than other areas. Instead, crime in Christendom reaches frightening proportions, unequaled outside its boundaries. These conditions turn many away from the Bible. Should they? Let us see.

The vital question that needs to be answered is this: Do Christendom's churches represent the Bible? Have they practiced its principles? Do they actually represent Christ, and has their influence on the nations been a genuinely Christian one? If the answer to these questions should prove to be "No," this would mean that they have perpetrated a great fraud on the people. It will be worth our while to make an honest examination of the facts.

CHRISTENDOM'S ATTITUDE TOWARD THE BIBLE

It is true that the Bible has had its widest circulation in the lands of Christendom. Most members of Christendom's churches have a copy. But does the mere possession of a book mean that the person has read it? Even if he has read it, does that mean he believes it? And even though he may claim to believe it, does that mean that he practices what the book teaches? To the contrary, the book may actually condemn what the person does.

Just how much is the Bible read in Christendom? In 1961, the *Yomiuri Shimbun* newspaper of Tokyo quoted the general secretary of the United Bible Societies as saying:

> "Millions of additional people are acquiring Bibles these days, but the book isn't being read much—except by non-Christians."—June 11, 1961.

The prominent religious magazine *The Christian Century* of September 5, 1962, put the matter even more bluntly, stating:

> "If we are really honest, would not a closed Bible, covered with dust and crammed with yellowing obituaries, be a better symbol of the actual state of Protestantism?"

Could people who do not read or study the Bible possibly be viewed as its representatives?

But why this apathy toward the Bible? What about the religious leaders, the clergy who teach the members of Christendom's churches? One might assume that they would show great interest in and appreciation for the Bible. Do they?

A Catholic newspaper, the *Luxemburger Wort*, of January 16, 1965, comments on the situation in Luxembourg:

> "Is it not a sad situation that . . . the overwhelming majority of our Catholics, yes, of our priests, never have completed the reading of the Bible, not even the New Testament?"

Is this lack of interest in the Bible within Christendom simply the result of negligence on the part of the church members and their clergy? No, the matter goes much deeper. It is not merely a question of interest. It is a question of belief. You yourself may have read statements like the following, for they are appearing with frequency in newspapers and magazines.

The Age of Melbourne, Australia, on February 18, 1967, quotes an Anglican rector as saying "the museum would be the best place for 80 per cent of the Old Testament."

Der Spiegel, a German newsmagazine, states:

> "For a number of professors [of theology] . . . their 'critical understanding' has made the Holy Scriptures into a collection of myths, symbols, fairy tales, poetry and pictures."—August 16, 1961.

In the United States, the leading branch of the Presbyterian Church announced that it does not consider the Bible "inerrant" (free from error).[52] And a *Time* magazine article[53] tells of a conservative Methodist theologian who teaches Michigan State college students that "the Bible is the greatest collection of mythology in the history of Western civilization."*

All this is not just a recent development. Back in 1929, in a survey of 500 theological students of the Baptist, Congregationalist, Episcopalian, Evangelical, Lutheran, Methodist and Presbyterian churches, the question was asked, "Do you believe that the Bible is wholly free from legend or myth?" Ninety-five percent of those answering said, "No."[54] Their answers reflected what they were being taught by older religious leaders. The principal difference in the situation today is that the clergymen of Christendom are becoming more and more open in revealing their disbelief in the Bible as the inspired Word of God.

WHAT OF THE GOD OF THE BIBLE?

By denying the inspiration of the Bible as the Word of God, these religious leaders, in effect, represent God as being mute, speechless, having no communication with mankind. Furthermore, it may be noted that they especially try to undermine faith in those parts of the Bible that describe God's taking action toward the earth and mankind on it, expressing his Sovereign power and will. They accept only those parts that might be explained on purely human terms. Thus, in effect, they would like to render God powerless as to human affairs.

It is little wonder, then, that some religious leaders go far beyond denying the Bible's truthfulness. These are the "God is dead" theorists, men who say that 'God is not present in history today.' Such a conclusion comes as a logical consequence of their rejection of the Bible as His

* Incidentally, the Bible is not a product of "Western civilization" but was written mainly in the Middle East.

inspired Word. Who are the advocates of the "God is dead" theory?

Canadian clergyman E. Harrison tells us in his book *A Church Without God:*

> "Werner Pelz, who entitled a book *God Is No More,* is a Church of England vicar; . . . Father Jackson, who says, 'If there is a God, we can't speak of him as a supreme being,' is a university chaplain; Thomas Altizer, who wrote *The Gospel of Christian Atheism,* is an Associate Professor of Bible Studies at an American university; I am on the staff of an Anglican parish in Toronto. I claim to be a Christian and an Anglican; yet I can say, in all seriousness, that THERE IS NO GOD." —1966, p. 39.

These men are not a rare exception among Christendom's clergymen. A report of the *National Observer* states: "A 'God is dead' mood pervades the thought of 90 percent of the Protestant theologians under 40."[55] And yet these clergymen call themselves "Christian"!

WHERE THE CLERGY STAND ON BIBLE MORALITY

The churches of Christendom have long professed to be the guardians of public morality. But are the religious leaders actually interested in seeing Bible principles applied? In this time of social breakdown, divorce, delinquency and violent crime, do they recognize the Bible as a real force for morality and support its high standards of conduct? What do they themselves say?

First, let it be noted that there is no haziness about the Bible's moral standards. The apostle Paul, for example, wrote:

> "What! Do you not know that unrighteous persons will not inherit God's kingdom? Do not be misled. Neither fornicators, nor idolaters, nor adulterers, nor men kept for unnatural purposes, nor men who lie with men, nor thieves, nor greedy

persons, nor drunkards, nor revilers, nor extortioners will inherit God's kingdom."—1 Corinthians 6:9, 10.

The Bible is very clear in limiting sexual intercourse to married persons. It plainly says: "Flee from fornication," "Abstain from fornication," "Let . . . the marriage bed be without defilement, for God will judge fornicators and adulterers." (1 Corinthians 6:18; 1 Thessalonians 4:3; Hebrews 13:4) How well do Christendom's church leaders represent the Bible's teachings in this regard?

With ever-increasing frequency religious leaders are advocating what is called the "new morality." What is this? Joseph Fletcher of an Episcopal theological school explains that "there is nothing against extra-marital sex as such, in this ethic, and in *some* cases it is good."[56] Roman Catholic theologian Eugene Hillman expresses the belief that polygamy "can serve good and constructive social purposes."[57]

Such men realize that their statements clash with those of the Bible. This is shown in an article entitled "Understanding Sex in the Age of the Pill," in *The Christian Century* magazine of January 8, 1969. The author, Presbyterian minister Gordon Clanton, states:

> "In the time of Jesus and throughout the nearly two millenniums of the church's life the teaching that sex should be reserved for marriage was sound, . . . But such a sweeping rule is no longer needed. . . .
>
> "For some time now theologians of 'liberal bent' have been hinting at the emergence of a 'new morality.' They have been brave enough to say that nonmarital sex is not necessarily wrong. Now we must go further and proclaim that, properly under-

stood and lovingly practiced, sex outside of marriage is indeed a positive good."

Identifying Biblical standards with what he calls "pre-Pill morality," minister Clanton goes on to say:

"The church should be seeking to weaken rather than strengthen the hold of pre-Pill morality on society."

If ministers seek to weaken rather than strengthen the power of Biblical teachings on the people, how can they possibly be viewed as representing the Bible? Nor are these isolated cases. *Time* magazine reports that this religious view of morality "claims an impressive array of advocates."—January 21, 1966.

As we have already noted at 1 Corinthians 6:9, 10, homosexuality is also strongly condemned in the Bible. But what stand do the clergy take on this? Have you not read news reports like the following in recent years?

On February 12, 1966, the New York *Times* carried a report on British legislation to repeal criminal penalties against homosexual acts by consenting adults. The report stated:

"Churches have been in the forefront of the demand for reform. The Church of England and Roman Catholic and Methodist groups have all called for adoption of the [repeal] recommendation."

The following year the same newspaper reported on a meeting of Episcopalian bishops in New York, stating:

"Ninety Episcopalian priests generally agreed yesterday that the church should classify homosexual acts between consenting adults as 'morally neutral' and acknowledge that in some cases such acts may even be a good thing. . . . The Episcopal

Diocese of San Francisco has openly supported an organization of homosexuals."—November 29, 1967.

From The Hague, Netherlands, comes the following:

"Two male homosexuals were secretly 'married' by a Roman Catholic priest in Rotterdam last week. . . . There is also a strong movement within the Roman Catholic priesthood to consider homosexual relationships in the same light as those between members of the opposite sex."[58]

It cannot be argued that this is just the personal view of an isolated priest or minister here and there. The newspaper *De Gelderland* of June 14, 1968, reported on a meeting of about 260 Catholic and Protestant clergymen from various countries meeting in Zeist, the Netherlands. The conclusion arrived at by these religious leaders was: "It is necessary to strive at a complete integration of the homosexual neighbor into the church as a group."

While not every clergyman approves of homosexuality, yet there is a strong trend in that direction in many lands. But how does the Bible describe homosexuality and its advocates? There is no mistaking its position:

"They became empty-headed in their reasonings . . . Although asserting they were wise, they became foolish and . . . exchanged the truth of God for the lie . . . That is why God gave them up to disgraceful sexual appetites, for both their females changed the natural use of themselves into one contrary to nature; and likewise even the males left the natural use of the female and became violently inflamed in their lust toward one another, males with males, working what is obscene and receiving in themselves the full recompense, which was due for their error."—Romans 1:21-27.

Someone may say, "Well, I have never heard my minister make statements like those quoted."

Perhaps not, but have you *asked him* what his stand is on these matters? And even though many ministers may not agree with those quoted, where are their voices of incensed protest? Where do we hear or read of them loyally defending the Bible against its enemies? And what of the church organizations that allow men such as those quoted to continue as their ordained representatives? Can those church organizations of Christendom disclaim responsibility? Does not the Bible forewarn that "a little leaven ferments the whole lump" and that a "good tree cannot bear worthless fruit"?—Galatians 5:9; Matthew 7:18.

"But such a course, representing oneself to be a minister of God and his Word, and then denying the power of both—this would be hypocrisy!" you might say. And you would not be alone in saying it. Even Christendom's clergy have said it about themselves. Note what Bishop Austin Pardue, of the Protestant Episcopal Diocese of Pittsburgh, admits:

> "Our hypocrisy is not deliberate, but convenient. The vicious malady of our orthodox American denominations comes from the corroding acids of disbelief which have watered down our convictions to the point where much of our religion has become a matter of mere custom and tradition."[59]

Really, how different is this situation from that in the time when Jesus was on earth? When addressing the religious leaders of that time, Jesus plainly told them that they had 'made the word of God invalid because of their tradition.' He compared them to "whitewashed graves, which outwardly indeed appear beautiful but inside are full of dead men's bones and of every sort of uncleanness," adding: "In that way you also, outwardly indeed, appear righteous to men, but inside you are full of hypocrisy and lawlessness." (Matthew 15:1-9; 23:27, 28) How would Jesus describe men who do these same things today? Do such clergymen really represent God and his Word?

WHAT HAS BEEN THEIR MOTIVE?

Should the actions of churches of Christendom and their religious leaders make us doubt that the Bible is the Word of God? To the contrary, it should increase our confidence in that Word. Why? Because the Bible not only condemns their practices but also foretold that they would engage in such hypocrisy. It also identifies clearly the motives that have led them to act contrary to the Bible and the teachings of Christianity.

Nineteen hundred years ago, the apostle Paul foretold such apostasy. He said:

> "For there will be a period of time when they will not put up with the healthful teaching, but, in accord with their own desires, they will accumulate teachers for themselves to have their ears tickled." —2 Timothy 4:3.

The clergy of Christendom have endeavored to please their hearers in order that they might have large flocks and good financial support. In their quest for popularity, they have steadily relaxed Bible principles and forsaken its standards of righteousness. They have "watered down" the Word of God, like the ancient peddlers of wine, who added water to it to make it go farther. (2 Corinthians 2:17) Are such men and their church organizations the pillars of strength that they purport to be? Should the word of such men be counted as carrying any weight when they level charges against the Bible? Rather, their course betrays their lack of moral strength and their inability or unwillingness to hold to the high standards of the Bible.

In this regard, note these remarks of a minister of the First Universalist Church of Denver regarding Christendom's clergy:

> "We are rated by our denominations by the kinds of statistics we can accumulate—members and money, missions, financial support for our ecclesiastical superstructures.
>
> "In many ways the modern clergyman is little more than a parish prostitute. We quickly become 'organizational men'—by fitting into the system, we guarantee ourselves a lifetime job. By behaving ourselves, we know that we will move to larger churches and higher salaries. . . . As a result we are more interested in building up the church than in building men. . . . We quickly learn what people want to hear and we give it to them."[60]

The Bible foretold that "in the last days critical times hard to deal with" would come, and that men would have "a form of godly devotion but proving false to its power." Christendom's churches and their leaders today retain only the "form." The "power" of God's Word and its message is obviously missing among them. The Bible's counsel is: "From these turn away."—2 Timothy 3:1-5.

HOW THE APOSTASY GOT STARTED

This deviation from the standards and teachings of the Bible has its roots in the early centuries of the Common Era. Jesus Christ, the founder of Christianity, knew that this apostasy would come and foretold it when giving one of his parables or illustrations. He likened true Christians, the "sons of the kingdom," to fine grains of wheat sown in a field, which is "the world." But then, Jesus said, God's adversary Satan the Devil would oversow that field with "weeds"—the "sons of the wicked one." God would let both the "wheat" and the "weeds" grow until the "harvest season." Then he would make the "wheat" and the "weeds" clearly distinguishable and would have his harvesters gather in the "wheat" and destroy the "weeds."—Matthew 13:24-30, 36-43.

Jesus' disciples likewise foretold this apostasy. The apostle Paul forewarned Christians in Asia Minor:

> "I know that after my going away oppressive wolves will enter in among you and will not treat the flock with tenderness, and from among you yourselves men will rise and speak twisted things to draw away the disciples after themselves."—Acts 20:29, 30.

The historical evidence is that such wolfish men led many away from Bible standards into worldliness. Christ Jesus had plainly stated, "My kingdom is no part of this world." The disciple James condemned as "adulteresses" those who sought the friendship of the world, and added: "Whoever, therefore, wants to be a friend of the world is constituting himself an enemy of God." (John 18:36; James 4:4) Apostate Christians ignored these Biblical teachings. In the fourth century C.E., Emperor Constantine of Rome was supposedly "converted."* This opened the way for the apostates from Christianity to gain worldly favors. As M'Clintock and Strong's *Cyclopœdia* relates:

* Subsequent to this "conversion," Constantine approved the killing of his youthful nephew, his wife Fausta, and his own son Crispus.

> "The simplicity of the Gospel was corrupted; pompous rites and ceremonies were introduced; worldly honors and emoluments were conferred on the teachers of Christianity, and the kingdom of Christ in a good measure converted into a kingdom of this world."—Vol. 2, p. 488.

This was not Biblical Christianity. It was counterfeit Christianity, a fraud. The Bible shows that Christ Jesus had turned down control of the political kingdoms of this world offered him by God's adversary, Satan. (Matthew 4:8-11) Taking an opposite course, in the fifth century C.E. Pope Leo I proclaimed:

> "I will revive government once more upon this earth; not by bringing back the Caesars, but by declaring a new theocracy, by making myself the vicegerent of Christ, . . . Not a diadem, but a tiara will I wear, the symbol of universal sovereignty, before which barbarism shall flee away, and happiness be restored once more."[61]

The result was—no, not happiness, but corruption, superstition and bloodshed. The Dark Ages descended upon Western Europe. The Bible practically disappeared in the languages of the common people. This was the period, not when the Bible was read most, but when the Bible was read least. Read for yourself in any reputable encyclopedia what this turning away from Bible standards brought upon the people during that period of Christendom's greatest power, wealth and influence. Read about the Crusades that began in the eleventh century C.E., as church leaders sent wave after wave of pillaging, ravaging hordes against the East. Read of the Crusaders' capture of Jerusalem and the resulting bloodbath as Mohammedans and Jews were mercilessly slaughtered. How well these "Holy Wars" are summed up by a modern historian in *The Story of Civilization:*

> "In short, the Crusades were an exhibition of unbridled, unprincipled, unrestrained savagery in the name of Christ."—P. 587.

As you read, ask yourself: Were these armies of Christendom fulfilling the Bible prophecy at Isaiah 2:4? This states:

> "They will have to beat their swords into plowshares and their spears into pruning shears. Nation will not lift up sword against nation, neither will they learn war any more."

Were they following genuine Christianity as taught by the apostles? The apostle Paul writes:

> "Though we walk in the flesh, we do not wage warfare according to what we are in the flesh. For the weapons of our warfare are not fleshly, but powerful by God for overturning strongly entrenched things."—2 Corinthians 10:3, 4.

And keep in mind this same Bible teaching as you read what Roman Catholic authorities state in the booklet *The Truth About the Inquisition:*

> "The Church cannot escape responsibility for the use of torture nor for the burning of victims at the stake. . . . we frankly acknowledge the responsibility of the popes in the use of torture and in the burning of thousands of heretics at the stake. Their sanctioning of such cruel and brutal measures is unquestionably one of the blackest stains on the record of the Holy Office and will remain to the end of time a cause of obloquy and shame upon the papacy."—Pp. 47, 49.

The Protestant Reformation, beginning in the sixteenth century, brought an increase in Bible reading for a time. This was accompanied by many improvements in education and in legislation, providing for greater justice and tolerance. But the religious leaders of the Protestant churches did not heed the Bible exhortation given by the apostle Paul at 1 Corinthians 1:10-13:

> "Now I exhort you, brothers, through the name of our Lord Jesus Christ that you should all speak in agreement, and that there should not be divisions among you, but that you may be fitly united in the same mind and in the same line of thought. . . . Does the Christ exist divided?"

They not only disagreed among themselves but also held on to many teachings that contradicted the Bible, including that of a Trinity of gods, all equal, all coeternal, all of the identical substance. Yet Jesus said, "The Father is greater than I am." (John 14:28; 5:19, 30) They retained the doctrine of a burning hell of literal fire in which God is supposed to torture the wicked. Yet the Bible says that the dead "are conscious of nothing at all," and that the "wages sin pays is death," not eternal torment. (Ecclesiastes 9:5, 10; Romans 6:23) And although they rejected the authoritarian rule of the Papacy, they still maintained a division between clergy and laity. Yet Jesus told his disciples not to have titled positions, saying that "all you are brothers," and that whoever "exalts himself will be humbled."—Matthew 23:8-12.

Nor did those Protestant church leaders divorce themselves from alliances with the political state. They blessed and supported the political governments in their wars of aggression and in their empire building. Because of the connection of Christendom's churches with colonialism, their missionaries often meet up with hatred in foreign nations.

Have you heard of the "Opium Wars" prosecuted by nations of Christendom against China during the middle of the nineteenth century?

Read this description from *Life* magazine of September 23, 1966:

> "In a series of engagements they [the British] proved that nobody—least of all the Imperial Government [of China], could stop them from peddling narcotics, or any other profitable trade goods, wherever a good market existed. . . .
>
> "Four thousand tons [of opium] a year entered China in the 1850s. . . .
>
> "The main result of the Opium War was the opening of five treaty ports where foreign merchants could live and do business under their own consuls. Missionaries were permitted too, . . .
>
> "The Westerners wanted still more concessions. . . . France and Britain then mounted a joint expedition and shot their way into the [Chinese] capital in 1860. . . . In the end China was compelled to open more ports, pay the expenses of the expedition and accept Western legations. They also gave missionaries access to the entire interior, thus sowing seeds that would sprout into the bitterly anti-Christian Boxer Uprising 40 years later."

Consider, too, the statement made by Methodist minister Gabriel Setiloane at the All-Africa Church Conference held in Uganda in 1963. He said:

> "The advance of the Church in Africa has gone hand in hand with the Adventurer, the Explorer, the Colonizer and even the Imperialist. The hand that planted the Cross . . . on this continent was not that of the priest or apostle. It was the blood-stained hand of the soldier. . . . Even up to this century the Church in this continent, in spite of remonstrations to the contrary, has not been able to tear itself loose from the cords of Caesar's robes."

It is, then, a grave error to appraise the Bible on the basis of Christendom's history, its teachings, its practices. How true this is, is made evident in the following admission by noted churchman Harry Emerson Fosdick:

"Our Western history has been one war after another. . . .

"With one corner of our mouth we have praised the Prince of Peace and with the other we have glorified war. So well have we succeeded in blending Christ and carnage, the Gospel and organized slaughter, that recently a missionary in an Oriental country, after an address upon Christian goodwill, was taken aside by a native, who said, 'You must know that the educated people of this country look upon Christianity as a warring, blood-spilling religion.' "[62]

Not Christianity based on the Bible, but Christendom with its divided churches must bear the guilt for prejudicing millions of persons against the Bible. Yet it is this very book that contains God's condemnation of Christendom's course and proves Christendom to be a colossal fraud perpetrated in the name of Christianity! For to Christendom and her churches the words apply:

"They publicly declare they know God, but they disown him by their works."—Titus 1:16.

CHRISTENDOM REAPS WHAT SHE HAS SOWN

The "harvest" time foretold in the Bible has arrived. The difference between the "weeds" or counterfeit Christians sown by God's adversary, and the "wheat" or genuine Christians is now clearly distinguishable. Christendom has proved to be, not a spiritual paradise producing the fruits of God's holy spirit, but a weed patch of disunity, faithlessness and unprincipled conduct. In many parts of the world she has produced only "rice Christians," persons who joined her churches for the material benefits they could get.

How true the Bible teaching!—

"God is not one to be mocked. For whatever a man is sowing, this he will also reap."—Galatians 6:7.

Having sown contrary to God's Word the Bible, Christendom is now reaping the consequences: serious internal strife, a grave lack of candidates for her seminaries, dwindling church membership, a steady loss of influence, public criticism for political meddling, and widespread delinquency and immorality. Having prostituted themselves to the political powers to gain influence with them, Christendom's churches cannot escape being classified as part of the harlot-like "Babylon the Great," the symbolical "great city that has a kingdom over the kings of the earth." (Revelation 17:1-6, 18) To Christendom, no less than to pagandom, apply the words:

> "Get out of her, my people, if you do not want to share with her in her sins, and if you do not want to receive part of her plagues. For her sins have massed together clear up to heaven, and God has called her acts of injustice to mind."—Revelation 18:4, 5.

If you want to be among those whom God calls "my people," you cannot look to Christendom for guidance concerning His Word nor for an example of what its teachings and principles are. But there are genuine Christians today, persons who believe the Bible is God's Word and are convinced of the rightness of its standards and principles, persons who strive to live by those principles and who are willing to die rather than violate them. They live in every part of the earth, and are of many races and nations, but they are at peace with one another, have love for one another and are united in unselfishly aiding those who seek to know the truth about God and His Word. What is the grand hope that unites them, and which they hold out to you? The final chapter of this book will tell you.

CHAPTER 14

The Bible, Your Guide to a Happy Future

HAVING considered the evidence, what is your conclusion? Is the Bible really the Word of God? The evidence says, Yes! Why, as we have seen, even the objections raised against it, when investigated, simply confirm the Bible's superiority to human wisdom.

What, then, do *you* believe? You have seen that the Bible answers major questions—questions otherwise unanswerable. You realize that scientists cannot reveal the origin of the universe or of our planet Earth and life upon it. Yet the Bible does. It explains why mankind is plagued with difficulties, disease and death. It shows how relief will come. The Bible is not a dead word but is alive with practical wisdom and sound guidance. And it calls for action—*now,* in order to enjoy a life of purpose and a happy future. Is that what you want?

Do you believe that the Creator of the universe has the wisdom and power to make things right on this planet? If so, then you will want to know his solution. And you will want to put yourself in harmony with it.

A NEW ADMINISTRATION FOR ALL THE EARTH

The Bible reveals the reason why man's rule of earth has proved so disillusioning. It makes clear that it was never Jehovah God's purpose that man should govern the earth independently of his Creator. (Jeremiah 9:23, 24; 10:23) That is why God's Son, Christ Jesus, taught men to pray to God:

> "Let your kingdom come. Let your will take place, as in heaven, also upon earth."—Matthew 6:10.

Do you pray for this? Then you should realize that God's answer to that prayer will mean the end of man-made governments. It will mean that the whole earth will be under one government, a heaven-based government: God's kingdom. —Daniel 2:44.

"Incredible!" some persons will say. And yet world leaders increasingly recognize the urgent need to have a unified control of earth's affairs. Like British historian Arnold J. Toynbee, they see that 'civilization has reached the point where the very continuity of the human race depends on the formation of World Government.'[63] They have even tried to lay the basis for it. They speak of it as their "dream."

But Jehovah God is not dreaming. The one government his Word promises for all mankind will succeed where international efforts have failed. Why? Because it has as its head, not imperfect, dying men, but God's own Son. And because it owes its power and authority, not to politics or militarism, but to the Supreme Sovereign, Jehovah God. (Daniel 7:13, 14, 27) Reading the hearts of men, Jehovah God will go to the root of human wrongdoing. (Jeremiah 17:9, 10) He will cause his Son to enforce earth wide the rule at Proverbs 2:21, 22:

> "The upright are the ones that will reside in the earth, . . . As regards the wicked, they will be cut off from the very earth; and as for the treacherous, they will be torn away from it."

Not just a few dictators or war criminals, but all human fomenters and supporters of unrighteousness will be cleaned out when God destroys all false religion and, thereafter, at God's war of Armageddon. (Revelation 17:5-18; 16:14-16; 19:11-21) More than that, God's Son will remove the invisible extraterrestrial influence that stimulates wrongdoing. No, we do not refer to some strange fleshly creatures inhabiting Mars or some other planet of outer space. We refer to the invisible forces the Bible identifies: Satan the Devil and his spirit associates. (Ephesians 6:12) You have seen the evidence in our day of their influence, provoking men to commit brutality and mass bloodshed such as are unknown even among animals. The King of God's government has the power to do what nuclear science never could: put such demonic forces out of action.—Hebrews 2:14, 15; Revelation 20:1-3.

ENDURING PEACE AND SECURITY

What will this cleansing operation bring for those granted survival? It will mean the end of war, the scrapping of all military programs. (Psalm 46:9) Think of the resulting benefits. The world now spends over $20,000,000 *an hour* on arms and armies. Nor is that all. As the New York *Times* commented:

> "[Since] at least four men must labor to keep one soldier armed, fed and supplied . . . an end to the arms race would enable 75,000,000 men to turn to peaceful tasks."[64]

Would you not rejoice to see that? But only God's government will provide the basis for total disarmament. Everyone who will survive to life under that righteous rule must first have fulfilled the requirement at Isaiah 2:4:

"They will have to beat their swords into plowshares and their spears into pruning shears. Nation will not lift up sword against nation, neither will they learn war any more."

"And what will keep crime from later rearing up its ugly head to mar earth's peace and good order?" someone may ask. The Kingdom government will see to that. (Isaiah 9:6, 7) As foretold, God's Son will direct earth's affairs, justly and fairly, but with strength.

"There will be enjoyment by him in the fear of Jehovah. And he will not judge by any mere appearance to his eyes, nor reprove simply according to the thing heard by his ears. And with righteousness he must judge the lowly ones, and . . . with the spirit of his lips he will put the wicked one to death."—Isaiah 11:3, 4.

Under his administration you will never again need to lock your door or fear for the safety of your loved ones. Not hidden electronic listening devices or concealed television cameras, but God's spirit, will be the deterrent for wrongdoing then. Its effect on human minds and hearts helps persons rid themselves of animalistic tendencies—to stop growling, snapping, tearing at one another. (Galatians 5:22, 23; James 3:13-18) Fostering this spirit, Christ's government will supply the highest education, focusing on knowledge of the Creator, his works, laws and purposes.—Isaiah 11:2, 6-9.

Would you enjoy as your neighbors men and women who sincerely love God with their whole heart and who love their fellowmen as themselves? Are you willing to be that kind of neighbor yourself? (Psalm 133:1; Matthew 22:37-39) Then you will want to be included in the educational program that God's Kingdom government offers.

AN EARTH-WIDE EDEN

You may have seen color photos of this planet as taken by astronauts from the region of the moon. They show why Earth is well described as a 'jewel in space.' Yet, today, here on earth's surface we see much that is unpleasant, ugly. Big cities befoul the air, fester with slums and breed frustration. Do you, then, personally rejoice at the Bible's promise that God will soon "bring to ruin those ruining the earth"?—Revelation 11:18.

Once Armageddon's storm has swept the planet clean of such elements, then earth's woods and meadows, mountains and valleys, lakes and streams will regain their natural beauty. Properly cultivated, the entire earth will become parklike, a garden of God. (Genesis 1:28; 2:8; Luke 23:43) Both men and animals will be at peace with one another. (Hosea 2:18) With Armageddon survivors seeking God's blessing and direction, the earth will produce in rich abundance. And God will keep his promise, recorded at Isaiah 25:6:

> "Jehovah of armies will certainly make for all the peoples . . . a banquet of well-oiled dishes, a banquet of wine kept on the dregs, of well-oiled dishes filled with marrow."

Earth's rule by God's Son guarantees that the pain and weakness of hunger and famine will never be known again.—Psalm 67:6.

HEALTHFUL ENJOYMENT OF LIFE—FOREVER

Today, despite its advances, medical science still fights a losing battle with disease. Human life is still short. Man just begins to learn and develop his knowledge and abilities when infirmities start to cut him down. Yet, by his prophet Isaiah, Jehovah God has given the promise that he will "actually swallow up death forever, and the Lord Jehovah will certainly wipe the tears from all faces." (Isaiah 25:8) Do you find this difficult to believe? Then, take a moment to consider God's creation. Look at the trees, such as the sequoias or the cypress trees, some of which live for thousands of years. Is it not logical that the Creator originally made intelligent man to live far longer than mere vegetation? God the Creator gave the marine creature known as the starfish the ability to grow a whole new arm if one is broken off. Cannot he also restore human bodies to perfect health and completeness? Certainly he can. In fact, he has already demonstrated this. How? By the power he granted his Son when on earth among ailing mankind.

Blind eyes, deaf ears, lame limbs, and diseases as dreaded as leprosy all yielded to the God-given power of Jesus Christ. You can read the historical testimony of this in the Bible. (Matthew 4:23; Mark 5:25-34; 7:31-37; Luke 5:12, 13; 13:11-13; John 9:1-32) He used no human or animal donors for organ transplants. Instead he restored to health the very organs or body parts afflicted. Will you seek to be among those who will benefit when he applies this regenerative power under his Kingdom rule? No illness or health problem will resist his cure. For, through the merit of his ransom sacrifice, he will remove inherited sin and imperfection, which are the cause of disease and of old age and death.—1 Corinthians 15:25, 26; Revelation 21:4.

And what of all those who have died and whose bodies molder in the dust of the earth? The Bible declares God's purpose to empty gravedom of its victims. (Revelation 20:12, 13) That is why Jesus said:

> "Do not marvel at this, because the hour is coming in which all those in the memorial tombs will hear [my] voice and come out."—John 5:28, 29.

The resurrections Jesus performed while on earth, including one of a man four days dead, assure us that he has that power.—John 11:43, 44.

Those resurrected will also have the opportunity to gain everlasting life. (Revelation 20:12-15) Do you find these Bible promises heartwarming? Who could not feel drawn to God upon realizing how he will cause past tragedies, resulting from war, murder, disease and even fatal accidents, to be canceled out by means of the resurrection?

However, you may soberly ask, "Under such conditions, with perfect health restored, what will prevent the earth from becoming overpopulated?" In the first book and first chapter of the Bible, God's purpose for the earth is made clear. To the original human pair he gave the commission:

> "Be fruitful and become many and fill the earth." —Genesis 1:28.

You may be sure that God is not like the person who makes a container and then foolishly tries to put more into it than it will contain. The Creator gave humans their reproductive powers. As their heavenly Father, he is able to direct or control the use of those powers so that his earthly family comfortably fills, but never outgrows, its home.—Isaiah 40:12-14.

A TIME FOR DECISION

Any normal person wants life under prosperous and happy conditions. But how many want life under God's Kingdom government? How many are willing to bring their life into harmony with Bible standards? Many in our day are not. But what about you?

The choice God gave, through Moses, to the people of Israel is the same choice he places before you today:

> "I have put life and death before you, the blessing and the malediction; and you must choose life in order that you may keep alive, you and your offspring."—Deuteronomy 30:19.

You are free to make your own choice. But you should realize that Bible prophecies show the period of opportunity is running out. The time for decision is here. Do you believe the Bible as God's Word, or do you reject it? Or are you perhaps indifferent? Your attitude and course necessarily will influence others. If you are married, your mate and children inescapably are affected by what you do. What about them? Do you want to see them gain life in God's favor under his Kingdom rule? What are you willing to do to help them?

The Bible shows there is only one way to gain life in peace and happiness. It does not come from man, nor from pleasing man. Jesus Christ showed the primary step when he said:

> "This means everlasting life, their taking in knowledge of you, the only true God, and of the one whom you sent forth, Jesus Christ."—John 17:3.

How can you obtain such knowledge? Certainly not by attending the religious services of an organization that claims to carry on the worship of God but fails to aid its members to make a serious study of God's Word. Nor will you be drawn closer to mankind's Creator by attending a church where the Bible is perhaps quoted but its moral standards are not applied. As has been shown from the statements of its own spokesmen, Christendom does not represent the Bible. So you cannot expect to please God by turning to its churches for instruction or, if you are already a member, by continuing your affiliation with such organizations.

Nor can you win God's approval by isolating yourself. (Proverbs 18:1) The Bible plainly counsels us:

> "Let us consider one another to incite to love and fine works, not forsaking the gathering of ourselves together, as some have the custom, but encouraging one another, and all the more so as you behold the day drawing near."—Hebrews 10:24, 25.

But with whom will you gather for worship? Surely the wise course would be to seek out those who believe that the Bible is really the Word of God, and who then apply it in their lives and advocate it to others. Today there are hundreds of thousands of such persons in some two hundred lands and islands of the sea. They are known as the Christian witnesses of Jehovah. They are living now in harmony with their hope of enjoying life in God's new order. And they sincerely seek to help as many persons as they can to learn of that hope. That is why they now conduct hundreds of thousands of free home Bible studies throughout the earth. They will gladly help you and your family.

By contacting Jehovah's witnesses at the Kingdom Hall nearest you, or by writing the publishers of this book, you may receive a weekly visit from a qualified instructor. Using the Bible instruction book *The Truth That Leads to Eternal Life,* a six-month course will equip you with basic Bible knowledge in your own home. There is no charge for this service. But to benefit fully you must be willing to put forth an effort.

Jehovah God holds out the invitation to you to receive life-giving knowledge and act upon it. Through the Bible, he urges you:

> "My son, my law do not forget, and my commandments may your heart observe, because length of days and years of life and peace will be added to you. . . . Write them upon the tablet of your heart, and so find favor and good insight in the eyes of God and of earthling man. Trust in Jehovah with all your heart and do not lean upon your own understanding."—Proverbs 3:1-5.

The Bible can give true meaning to your life now as it has already done for a growing number of persons of all races, lands and tongues. Study it. Make it your guide. Live by it. Prove by your positive action that you believe the Bible really is the Word of God. Yes, in this time of decision, "choose life in order that you may keep alive, you and your offspring."

REFERENCES

1 *The Book of Books: An Introduction,* 1948, p. 194.
2 *The Junior Teacher's Guide,* Year 1, 1964, p. 4.
3 Toronto, Canada, *Daily Star,* October 14, 1967.
4 *The New Bible Dictionary,* 1963, p. 270.
5 *The Earth,* 1963, pp. 35, 38, 87.
6 *Earth's Shifting Crust,* 1958, p. 133.

7 *The Evidence of God in an Expanding Universe,* 1958, p. 34.
8 *Scientific American Reader,* 1953, p. 230.
9 *Science Problems,* 1958, p. 469.
10 *Prehistory and Earth Models,* p. 24.
11 *What Is Race?,* 1957, pp. 11, 12.
12 *Man's Most Dangerous Myth: the Fallacy of Race,* 1964, p. 83.
13 New York *Times,* December 30, 1968, p. 18.
14 *The Scientific Monthly,* August 1949, p. 71.
15 *The Scientific Monthly,* December 1957, p. 303.
16 *Earth's Shifting Crust,* 1958, p. 269.
17 Based on *Mammals of the World,* by Ernest P. Walker.
18 *The Encyclopedia of the Lutheran Church,* 1965, Vol. II; *New Catholic Encyclopedia,* 1967, Vol. II, p. 509.
19 *The Sun,* San Bernardino, Calif., October 19, 1967.
20 *Encyclopædia Britannica,* 1959, Vol. 13, pp. 698, 699.
21 *The Historical Evidences of the Truth of the Scripture Records,* 1862, p. 287.
22 *The World History of the Jewish People,* 1964, Vol. I, pp. 338, 339.
23 *Ancient Near Eastern Texts,* 1955, p. 288.
24 *A New Standard Bible Dictionary,* Funk and Wagnalls, 1936, p. 829.
25 *Ancient Near Eastern Texts,* 1955, p. 315.
26 *Archaeology and the Old Testament,* 1964, p. 270.
27 *Light from the Ancient Past,* 1959, p. 215.
28 *The Historical Evidences of the Truth of the Scripture Records,* 1862, pp. 25, 26.
29 *The Complete Works of Tacitus,* 1942, "The Annals," Book XV, par. 44.
30 *Beyond the Gospels,* 1957, p. 161.
31 *The New Bible Dictionary,* 1962, p. 11.
32 *Time,* July 4, 1955.
33 *The Sunday Express,* England, August 6, 1967.
34 *Telegraph-Journal* of Saint John, N.B., Canada, December 16, 1959.
35 *Archaeology and the Old Testament,* 1964, pp. 175, 176.
36 *The Encyclopedia Americana,* 1956, Vol. 22, p. 664.
37 *The Bible After Twenty Years of Archaeology,* 1954, p. 546.
38 *Babylon and the Old Testament,* 1956, p. 13.
39 *Josephus, the Jewish War,* Penguin Classics, 1967, p. 163.
40 *Ibid.,* p. 331.
41 *Ibid.,* p. 339.
42 *U.S. News & World Report,* November 27, 1967, p. 62.
43 *Today's Health Guide,* pp. 380, 412.
44 New York *Daily News,* June 1, 1968, p. 8.
45 The Bakersfield *Californian,* June 1, 1968.
46 *Today's Health Guide,* 1965, p. 188.
47 *Encyclopædia Britannica,* 1959, Vol. 14, p. 377.
48 *Reader's Digest,* April 1954, p. 9.
49 *Encyclopædia Britannica,* 1959, Vol. 23, p. 702.
50 *Reader's Digest,* December 1957, p. 212.
51 *The New Testament in the Original Greek,* 1957, p. 565.
52 New York *Times,* May 25, 1966.
53 *Time* magazine, February 4, 1966, p. 75.
54 *A Guide to the Religions of America,* 1955, p. 236.
55 *National Observer,* January 31, 1966.
56 *Commonweal,* January 14, 1966, p. 427.
57 Toronto, Canada, *Daily Star,* February 10, 1968.
58 New York *Post,* July 5, 1967.
59 Stated August 7, 1950.
60 The Denver *Post, Religious News Weekly,* December 10, 1966.
61 *Beacon Lights of History,* by John Lord, 1884, Vol. III, pp. 244, 245.
62 *The Modern Use of the Bible,* 1951, p. 204.
63 Associated Press Dispatch, New York, February 20, 1965.
64 New York *Times,* February 26, 1961.

WHAT THE BIBLE REALLY TEACHES

Would you like a brief, easy-to-understand presentation of what the Bible really teaches? It is available in the large-size, beautifully illustrated book *You Can Live Forever in Paradise on Earth.*

30 chapters
256 pages
Only $2.50

The Bible's
basic teachings
in logical order

Among the Bible truths discussed are:

- Why we are here
- Why we grow old and die
- What kind of place is hell?
- How can we be sure which religion God approves?
- How wicked spirits are misleading mankind
- Why has God permitted wickedness till now?
- Who go to heaven, and why?
- How to pray and be heard by God
- What the Bible says about building a happy family life

To obtain your copy of this attractive hardbound book postpaid, just send $2.50. Price subject to change.

Write to **Watchtower,** using an address from the next page.

A Bible You Can Easily Understand

The *New World Translation of the Holy Scriptures* is a Bible translation that you can easily understand. Why? Because difficult-to-understand, archaic language has been replaced with modern English throughout its pages. Readers and students of the Bible will find most satisfying this use of up-to-date language, as well as a generally uniform rendering of specific words of the original Greek and Hebrew text. Other helpful features: A concordance, marginal references, maps, and illuminating appendix.

Hardbound black cover with gilt title. Size: 6 3/4" x 4 7/8" x 1 3/8". Sent anywhere, postpaid, for $3.50. Price may be changed without notice.

Send your order to WATCHTOWER at any of these addresses:

ALASKA 99507: 2552 East 48th Ave., Anchorage. **AUSTRALIA:** Box 280, Ingleburn, N.S.W. 2565; Zouch Road, Denham Court, N.S.W. 2565. **BAHAMAS:** Box N-1247, Nassau, N.P. **BARBADOS:** Fontabelle Rd., Bridgetown. **BELIZE:** Box 257, Belize City. **BRAZIL:** Rodovia SP-141, Km 43, 18280 Cesario Lange, SP; Caixa Postal 92, 18270 Tatuí, SP. **CANADA L7G 4Y4:** Box 4100, Halton Hills (Georgetown), Ontario. **ENGLAND:** Watch Tower House, The Ridgeway, London NW7 1RN. **FIJI:** Box 23, Suva. **FRANCE:** 81 rue du Point-du-Jour, F-92100 Boulogne-Billancourt. **GERMANY, FEDERAL REPUBLIC OF:** Postfach 20, D-6251 Selters/Taunus 1. **GHANA:** Box 760, Accra. **GUAM 96921:** P.O. Box 20067, GMF, Guam. **GUYANA:** 50 Brickdam, Georgetown 16. **HAWAII 96814:** 1228 Pensacola St., Honolulu. **HONG KONG:** 4 Kent Road, Kowloon Tong. **INDIA:** Post Bag 10, Lonavla, Pune Dis., Mah. 410 401. **IRELAND:** 29A Jamestown Road, Finglas, Dublin 11. **JAMAICA:** Box 180, Kingston 10. **KENYA:** Box 47788, Nairobi. **LEEWARD ISLANDS:** Box 119, St. Johns, Antigua. **LIBERIA:** P.O. Box 171, Monrovia. **MALAYSIA:** 28 Jalan Kampar, Off Jalan Landasan, Kelang, Sel. **NEW ZEALAND:** 6-A Western Springs Road, Auckland 3. **NIGERIA:** P.O. Box 194, Yaba, Lagos State. **PAKISTAN:** 197-A Ahmad Block, New Garden Town, Lahore 16. **PANAMA:** Apartado 1835, Panama 9A. **PAPUA NEW GUINEA:** Box 113, Port Moresby. **PHILIPPINES, REPUBLIC OF:** P.O. Box 2044, Manila 2800; 186 Roosevelt Ave., San Francisco del Monte, Quezon City 3010. **PORTUGAL:** Av. D. Nuno Álvares Pereira, 11, P-2765 Estoril. **SIERRA LEONE:** Private Mail Bag 873, Freetown. **SOUTH AFRICA:** Private Bag 2, Elandsfontein, 1406. **SRI LANKA, REP. OF:** 62 Layard's Road, Colombo 5. **SWITZERLAND:** Ulmenweg 45; P.O. Box 225, CH-3602 Thun. **TRINIDAD:** Lower Rapsey Street & Laxmi Lane, Curepe. **UNITED STATES OF AMERICA:** 25 Columbia Heights, Brooklyn, N.Y. 11201. **ZIMBABWE:** 35 Fife Avenue, Harare.